The Actor Moves

The Actor Moves

Claudia N. Sullivan

McFarland & Company, Inc., Publishers
Jefferson, North Carolina, and London

British Library Cataloguing-in-Publication data are available

Library of Congress Cataloguing-in-Publication Data

Sullivan, Claudia N., 1950–
   The actor moves / by Claudia N. Sullivan.
     p. cm.
   Includes bibliographical references.
   Includes index.
   ISBN 0-89950-451-5 (lib. bdg. : 55# alk. paper) ∞
   1. Movement (Acting) 2. Theater—History. I. Title.
PN2071.M6S8 1990
792'.028—dc20   90-52507
                                             CIP

Manufactured in the United States of America

McFarland & Company, Inc., Publishers
  Box 611, Jefferson, North Carolina 28640

for Marc

Acknowledgments

The research for this book has taken many years. I have been helped by many individuals and groups, all of whom I thank.

This project would not have been started without the generous support provided by Dr. Sam Junkin of Schreiner College, Dr. Richard Knaub of the University of Colorado, and grants from Schreiner College Former Students Association. In addition I would like to mention: Charlotte Irey of the University of Colorado, Nancy Spanier of the Nancy Spanier Dance Theatre, Jennifer Martin of the University of Missouri at Kansas City, and Laurie Nomer and Mary Ann Parker of Schreiner College.

Finally, I am grateful to my mother, Evelyn Latimer, for her constant encouragement and assistance, and to my husband, Marc, for his love and his editorial skills.

Table of Contents

Acknowledgments   vii

Preface   xi

Introduction   1

1. The Legacy of the Sacred Circle   5

2. The Greeks: A Theatre of Spectacle   9

3. The Romans: Oratory and Entertainment   17

4. The Sixteenth and Seventeenth Centuries:
   Elizabethan and Rhetorical   23

5. The Eighteenth Century: Garrick and Diderot   29

6. Subjective Idealism: Romanticism and Delsarte   37

7. The Early Twentieth Century: Constantin Stanislavski   43

8. Meyerhold's Biomechanics   51

9. Postmodern Trends: Jerzy Grotowski   65

10. The New Specialists of Movement   87

11. The Future of Movement Training   109

Chapter Notes   133

Bibliography   141

Index   147

Preface

The human desire to express ourselves has been with us since we first emerged from the cave and perhaps even before that. Consider the cave paintings at Lascaux, France. The renditions of bison were painted by someone with a keen sensitivity to the realistic duplication of the bison's body line, color, and confirmation. But why would primitive man have such a need for detail? For aesthetic appreciation, certainly not. But what if, as with our ancestors, your life and survival depended on your knowledge of every movement and action of that bison? You would study it and ponder it until you came to know it as well as you know yourself. In carefully and lovingly reproducing the animal's image on a cave wall, or in your own mimic body movements, you somehow form a mystical connection with the spirit, or idea, of the animal.

In my own imagination, as the first actor moved into the sacred circle he or perhaps she probably did not speak. Utterances or chants may have accompanied the sound of drumming or the clacking of bones together, but I think there was no dialogue or verbal exchanges between actors. This first actor was more than an actor; he was a shaman, or priest, and he could work magic. The magic of the first actor was worked through movement. He danced and stomped and raised his arms skyward to beckon the blessings of the gods on his clan.

In each actor today there is something that I like to think of as a symbolic memory of that first actor. As modern actors we observe and study in an effort to realistically reproduce the dramatic image. We

enter the sacred circle (now the modern stage) and we still endeavor to
work mystical, magical acts. But we seem to have lost that all-important
connection with our bodies as our most important expressive instrument. Our ancient predecessors had it because they had no other expressive tools; only the movements of the body were the expression.
Perhaps our modern society is too rushed and we do not have enough
time to establish the mind/body/character connection. We may have
placed too much importance on the dramatic word and, if we get our
lines right and the meaning is clear, that should be enough for an effective characterization.

Possibly we do not know our bodies well enough. This seems im-
probable in an age of scientific breakthroughs and our preoccupation
with body image. Since the advent of psychology as an accepted science
we have become more attuned to how we *feel*, rather than how those
feelings are being expressed in gesture, movement, and mannerism. I
have written this book in order to discover some answers for the modern
actor as he or she prepares for a role, and then trains the mind, body,
and voice for the craft of acting.

My interest in movement for the actor began when I was a young
student of ballet. I remember watching Dame Margot Fonteyn dance in
Dallas in the mid–1960s. Her dance was more than the perfect execution
of technical combinations and I began to realize the potential power of
the expressive body. As my interest expanded into theatre and acting I
tried to capture feeling in actions first. But this seemed an impossible
task. So much emphasis has been placed on the words, the lines. "Make
sense of the lines," we were told. My early training included mime work
and movement exercises designed to increase strength, flexibility, and
awareness. But the movement training was not integrated with the vocal
work and character analysis. My fellow students and I were examples of
the loss of movement connection.

As I began to teach acting and direct plays I again faced the same
problem, but this time from the instructor's point of view. How can you
teach the movement connection to students? How can you help them
to discover it within themselves? Movement texts have been helpful for
specific problems. They offer examples of exercises which increase body
awareness, flexibility, strength, creative imagination, relaxation, and
period styles of movement. Yet few books on movement training

attempt to explain how we acquired our present attitudes on movement and movement training. *The Actor Moves* provides an overview of the use and importance of the actor's body since earliest times. A study of the history of acting will reveal changing attitudes with respect to the use of movement both in training and performance.

Any student of acting must also be a student of human movement since so much of any performance is at once inwardly connected to physical action and outwardly manifested in posture, gesture, facial expression, and mannerism. In order to study movement for the actor we must first begin to understand and accept the nature of the primitive ritual — its role in the life of ancient humans and its function as the wellspring from which theatre and drama were drawn. We should skip far ahead and learn too how the Greeks took ancient ritual and formalized it into what is today the highest quality of classical art. The leap from Quintilian to the rhetorical acting of the seventeenth century may seem a bit large in scope, but it is this connection between the Roman orator and the restrained style of the seventeenth century which made way for the most profound changes in acting. In succeeding centuries crucial theoretical and aesthetic questions have been raised, few or none of which have been answered to this day.

No history of acting and stage movement would be complete without giving attention to François Delsarte, Constantin Stanislavski, Vsevolod Meyerhold, and Jerzy Grotowski. In *The Actor Moves* I have discussed these practitioners in light of their contributions to movement theory and movement training for the actor. In addition, I found it necessary to include several movement specialists who did not come primarily from a theatrical background. Since the 1960s a variety of movement and body training approaches have gained acceptance in actor training programs — both in professional schools as well as university departments. Among the most widely used are Moshe Feldenkrais' Body Awareness; F.M. Alexander's Alexander Technique; and Rudolf Laban's Effort/Shape theory.

The modern actor is called upon, perhaps more now than at any time in history, to have a complete and immediate command of his physical, vocal, and intellectual instrument. The competition is fierce and jobs are scarce. Likewise, the actor trainer or director is especially concerned with the quality of training an actor receives, as it so strongly affects the finished product — the performance. *The Actor Moves* is written to fulfill two purposes: first, to provide background on specific aspects of the history of theatre — namely the movement training and movement styles of actors of the past. (What influenced the movement styles of the past and how were they related to other styles which preceded or proceeded from them?) Second, to suggest alternative movement theories which may complement present components in use in the classroom or rehearsal studio.

The Actor Moves is for actors, directors, movement specialists, and students of the theatre. It is my hope that it provides a unique point of view on an aspect of acting of which too little is written. Actors may speak their speeches trippingly off their tongues but they do not fully act until they move.

Introduction

The actor's body constitutes his instrument, his medium, his chief means of creative expression — that is a commonplace on which performers and spectators alike have readily agreed.... [C]onceptions of the human body drawn from physiology and psychology have dominated theories of acting from antiquity to the present. The nature of the body, its structure, its inner and outer dynamics, and its relationship to the larger world that it inhabits have been the subject of diverse speculation and debate.[1]*

The three areas essential to all actors are the mind (emotions), the voice, and the body. Yet, as Joseph Roach states in *The Player's Passion*, a debate has raged since earliest times over the importance, use, and training of the actor's instrument: his physical presence on the stage. For most of Western history, actor training and performance have focused on the voice as the prime means of expression. It was not until the nineteenth century that actors began to conduct research into the psychology of the roles they played. Prior to that time elocution, rhetoric, and vocal range were dominant in the actor's training and education. The value of the actor's body, on the other hand, was considered important, but important only in the sense that he appear graceful, elegant, and suitable for the conventions of the day. A radical change came in the late eighteenth century, a change which affected acting and acting theories, and which opened the way for an acceptance of the actor's body as the central focus of character personification.

See Chapter Notes, beginning on page 133.

1

The modernization of the physical sciences, their subsequent dis-
entanglement from ancient antiquity, helped eighteenth century
theorists for the first time to interpret the actor's emotions from outside
the framework of classical rhetoric. . . . The time honored philosophical
and scientific issues of the relationship of mind and body . . . [underlie]
the crucial questions of daily professional significance to the actor,
among them movement, gesture, characterization, motivation, concentration, imagination and memory.[2]

Questions which faced actors of hundreds of years ago still face actors of today. We have added more information and knowledge, more
theories and methods to our understanding of the actor's role and bodily
instrument, yet we still seek a clear definition to a prime aesthetic concern: How should the actor's body be trained, and how is it best utilized
during performance? The questions concerning stage movement are
reflected in the growing interest in movement training for the actor,
especially in the United States.

The theatre of the Western world has bequeathed an important
legacy to contemporary actors, directors, theatre aestheticians, and
theatre historians. This legacy is rich with ideas that have developed
from a basic need and desire to ritualize our experiences. Through the
passing of centuries and the growing sophistication of civilization we
have altered our rituals. No longer do we perform out of a sense of
cosmic survival. Today we seek entertainment, insight, and a place for
creative expression. Yet, today's actors act in much the same way as did
our ancestors. Actors today don makeup and costume; they memorize
actions and words. They struggle to invoke the "spirit" of the role
through inspiration, manipulation, concentration, or sheer rote
memory. Virtually all techniques, methods, systems, and theories have
been put to use at some time in one theatre or another. So, why do we
continue to search, to explore, to experiment, and to try to develop a
more effective way of "invoking the muse?" Man is an analytical and intellectual creature and as such, he is interested in, and bound to, the
mystical and magical experience of the theatre.

There are movement theories, movement specialists, movement
texts, and movement models, yet there still does not exist a generally
accepted philosophy dealing with the technique and goals of movement
training for the actor. Before we can state what movement training is,

it might be more appropriate to state what movement training is not.
It is not:

> mime, ballet, modern dance, jazz dance, T'ai Chi, karate, physical
> education, rolfing, fencing, stage combat, Alexander technique, acting,
> effort/shape. . . . However, almost all of the pioneers and teachers of
> movement for the actor's training have begun as students of one or
> several of these disciplines because there were no training programs for
> the actor.[3]

Movement for actor training may encompass a wide variety of
physical as well as psychophysical techniques, but it remains a discipline
which promotes, invites, encourages, and develops actors in the area of
stage movement.

Ideally, movement for actor training should lend itself to a more
integrated approach to character study. Movement training should provide exercises through which the actor may strengthen, focus and free
the body from personal mannerisms and open the actor to the physical
and psychophysical aspects of the character. Movement training also
should allow for the application of technique through which the actor
can explore and perform any character in any style from any period.

> Movement training must provide the actor with a means for finding and
> developing whatever is needed in movement for *any* production, *any*
> style or character.
> No strange style, whatever avant-garde or obscure historical, will
> long puzzle the actor who is in touch with a methodology for finding
> the essence of the needed movement. Having found the essence, it is a
> challenging but not difficult task to develop this beginning and to live
> in this movement—to breathe with it and to speak with ease, to feel an
> availability, a fulfillment, a physical logic.[4]

There exists a wide range of voiced needs from those involved in
movement training, yet there is little published information available
when compared to the volumes printed in the fields of speech and diction. Much of the existing library on movement training consists of pure
theory with little practical implementation of those theories.

> Increased interest in the physical aspects of the actor's art has resulted
> in a growing curiosity about movement training programs of the past.

> The American theatre offers little background in the field.... When
> ... training was given, it most often took the form of classes in ballet
> or modern dance, or, less frequently, mime. Acting texts printed in the
> United States after 1900 include little material on the physical formation
> of the performer.[5]

Until the 1960s there was little, if any, published work which solely focused on movement training for the actor. During the decade of the 1970s a number of new texts were published which specifically focused on movement training. Chiefly among these were: *Movement Training for Stage and Screen* by Jean Sabatine, *Movement for the Performing Artist* by Joseph Penrod, and Nancy King's *Theatre Movement: The Actor and His Space*. The presence of these authors' works is a hopeful sign in a field which needs research and publication. Academic research in the field is continuing to show improvement.

The actors, directors, and dramatic trainers of today may be waiting for the definitive outline of a movement training program suited for all actors in any role, in any play, but it simply does not exist. It cannot exist. No single approach can hope to meet the needs of all actors in all situations. Humans are too diverse and complex, and the range of today's theatrical production is demanding and varied. What we can best hope for is a clear understanding of the most significant movement theories and how they can be synthesized into a divergent program or philosophy which will be of use to the contemporary actor.

1. The Legacy of the Sacred Circle

The theatricalization of human body movement began as soon as the ritual of theatre experience emerged in ancient dramatic tradition. Research and sociological speculation support the idea that performed rites involved human movement in the form of ritualistic dances, symbolic gestures or other type of pantomimic action in an effort to glorify or appease the gods, to educate the novice members of the community in the traditions and values of the community, or to insure the future of the community. Benjamin Hunningher clearly states this in his essay "The Origin of the Theater."

> Nearly all primitive people enact the regular changes of nature in their plays, clearly intending to bring under their control elements which they do not dominate and, if necessary, to correct them. In such enactment, the element of play retreats gradually into the background and presentation comes to the fore, to such an extent that we may even speak of vicarious representation in dramatic action. So it coincides with ritual.[1]

The myths and rituals of ancient society served many purposes. They were used to educate, to establish rites of passage from one period of life to another, and to insure the blessings of nature in the form of a bountiful harvest, a successful hunt, or fertility in human and beast. But more important, the ritual bound people to nature. The ritual was proof that humans and nature were in accordance with one another. If death came, or the crops failed, or the hunters came home empty handed, it was no fault of any cosmic force. It was the fault of the performance of the ritual.

Perhaps the first ritual came about accidentally. An ancient hunter is on his way to a kill. He cuts himself and drops of his own blood fall on his spear, and as he bends to drink water from a spring his spear falls in. A short time later he sees his prey. He strikes and kills. Was the kill a result of magical powers in his own blood or the water of the spring? He does not know but the next day he repeats his actions and is successful again. He now believes in the magical powers — a *ritual* is born.

A *rite* is a specific action or part of a ritual. For example, a rite of passage is part of the overall ritual of becoming an adult. The rite of capturing the spirit or image of an animal, either in dress or action, is part of the ritual of the hunt. Unfortunately, no records of these ancient rites or rituals survive. Today we must imagine what they were like based on the anthropologist's findings.

Again in my own imagination, I see the earliest rites as primarily movement and action oriented. The movements performed as part of these rites were exact and fixed, since part of the function of a ritual was the careful replication of each movement.

> [N]othing so transports a person, so enables him to approach and enter into the Supernatural as the rhythm of a dance....
>
> In archaic societies usually the whole community dances, not just the able-bodied males. The dances are exact — a single misstep and the dance must be repeated from the beginning, to prevent the spirit from becoming confused and to preserve the order of the dance itself.[2]

Should any member of the community make a mistake the magic of the ritual was broken. The *taboo* became an important idea. A taboo was any action which broke the magic of the ritual. The observance of taboo was a top priority because the whole community was at risk. The ancients had no scientific knowledge; if any natural disaster, illness, or tragedy befell the clan it was most often due to the committing of a taboo.

Ancient rituals were a synthesized performance of religious, social, and disciplinary values. Those who took part in the ritual directly were the focus — the first actors — but the role of the audience was equally important. All members of the community had some function in the ritual.

Each moment of the ritual was carefully planned, including gestures, movement patterns, and spatial arrangements. The careful, detailed performance of the ritual was to insure what David Cole refers to as the *illud tempus*. This concept of the *illud tempus* reaffirms the sacred presence, the reality of the existence of a character. To the ancients this presence or character was the god or spirit. For the modern audience it is the realism of the presence of the dramatic character.

> The remarkable thing about the *illud tempus* is that whereas one might suppose it, of all eras, to have vanished irretrievably, it, in fact, can — unlike the merely historical periods which follow it — be made present again at any moment, by the performance of a ritual. . . .
>
> In a word, the *illud tempus* is not so much when it first occurred as where it is always happening. And further, since what is always happening is ever-accessible, the *illud tempus* has the potential to be, at any moment, among us.[3]

These ritualistic actions were performed time after time and in exact detail. They were passed on to each new generation, whose responsibility it then became to observe the movements carefully, and to imitate what they had seen so many times before. Most theorists accept that these primitive rituals were stylized and formalized over time.

> [T]heatre . . . gradually evolved out of dances that are primarily rhythmical and gymnastic or from imitation of animal movements or sounds. In each, it is in large part the virtuosity and grace of the performers that [are] valued, and supposedly these qualities are encouraged until they are elaborated into fully realized theatrical performances.[4]

The development of rites and rituals may have existed from the time of earliest man. Some scientists suggest this could be as early as 100,000 years ago. As the clan grew more complex and began to constitute a community, and as the community merged with other groups and formed a society, changes in the ritual were inevitable. The body of knowledge grew and with that knowledge came a relaxation in the exact adherence to the rites. In most cultures rituals continued to be performed but the performance was out of respect for the tradition of the ritual rather than the assertion that the ritual controlled events. Thus, the *myth* was born. For the purposes of a work on acting, a myth may be defined as a ritual which is performed but the performer no longer believes in the outcome as a result of the performance.

> Throughout the inhabited world, in all times and under every cir-
> cumstance, the myths of man have flourished; and they have been the
> living inspiration of whatever else may have appeared out of the ac-
> tivities of the human body and mind. . . . Religions, philosophies, arts,
> the social forms of primitive and historic man, prime discoveries in
> science and technology, the very dreams that blister sleep, boil up from
> the basic, magic ring of myth.[5]

Today we have evidence that ancient rituals were performed in
almost every culture from which we have gathered artifacts. The caves
at Lascaux, France, contain 600 paintings and over 1000 engravings of
our ancestor actors in their attempt to capture the spirit, life, and movement of those beings with which they shared the earth. Early American
Indian legends and dances have been passed on in a tradition which
brings us closer to the kinds of performances which occurred long ago.

The movements of the earliest actor must have been eloquent.
They were probably not inspired by humans, but were evocative of
animal grace, power, strength, and habit. The significance today of the
"acting" of the earliest actor is not in his performance but in his belief
that he was both the subject of the performance and the performance
itself.

2. The Greeks:
A Theatre of Spectacle

The major source of drama as known in the Western world today was Athens, Greece, in the fifth century B.C. These auspicious beginnings of written dramatic texts and festival performances were largely due to the texts provided by Aeschylus, Sophocles, Euripides, Aristophanes and their contemporaries whose works have not survived the times. These plays, together with the dramatic criticism of Aristotle's *Poetics* provide the foundation from which Western theatre has developed, evolved, and exists today.

Little direct evidence exists concerning the origins of theatre prior to the fifth century B.C. The earliest performances were part of the religious festival of the god Dionysus. The festival of Dionysus, held in the spring of the year, was an important ritual function in an ecstatic religion. The colorful and miraculous life of the god Dionysus inspired games, songs, poems, and odes in celebration of his gifts of wine, fertility, and rebirth. The consumption of the lifeblood of Dionysus (the wine) contributed to the ecstatic rapture of those carrying out the ritual. The mortal patrons of the god danced in the mountains near Delphi and were transported or lifted out of themselves into a kind of ritual connection with Dionysus. These early followers were the first "method" actors. Today we know that intoxication encourages one to behave in an uninhibited and unrestrained manner, yet for the ancient Greek the altered state of behavior was a direct result of the presence of the spirit of the god.

9

The art of the dramatic ritual required the actor to sublimate himself to the character or identity of the god (or demon, or spirit, or hero) that was the object of the ritual or play. This transformation from mere mortal to god or other characterization involved more than playing a part. Like the primitive predecessor, the Greek actor became the part through a belief in the actual presence of the idea or spirit of the god. The dancer-singer-actor was changed through *mimesis* into someone or something else.

The concept of imitation or mimesis has been a fundamental concern for the actor since ancient times. To what extent does the actor imitate, or are his emotions sincere and truly heart-felt? Are the actions and movements of the performer imitative of those observed in everyday life, or are they stylized, formal, or elegant? The first major work to explore these questions was written in the fourth century B.C. by Aristotle (384-322 B.C.). In his *Poetics,* Aristotle lends little advice on performance, costume, setting, or action. He does, however, have much to say concerning style and tragedy. On the subject of imitation Aristotle is very specific:

> Since the objects of imitation are men in action, and these men must be either of a high or a low type . . . , it follows these we must represent men either as better than in real life, or as worse, or as they are.[1]
>
> Tragedy, then, is an imitation of an action that is serious, complete, and of a certain magnitude; in language embellished with every kind of artistic ornament . . . in the form of dramatic action, not of narrative, through pity and fear effecting the proper purification of these emotions. . . .
>
> Again, tragedy is the imitation of an action, and an action implies personal actors, who necessarily possess certain distinctive qualities of character and thought; for it is by these that we form our estimate of their actions and these two—thought and character— are the natural causes from which their actions spring, and on their actions all success or failure depends.
>
> And life consists of action, and its end is a mode of activity, not a quality. Now character determines men's qualities, but it is their action that makes them happy or wretched. The purpose of action in the tragedy, therefore, is not the representation of character: character comes in as contributing to the action.[2]

The idea of mimesis and the relationship of art to life have long been a subject of debate. In fact, mimesis implies an absence. In the theatre, whether in an ancient, symbolic theatre or the modern theatre of entertainment, the prime focus is on the presence of the actor as character or the performer as spirit. Mimesis represents the absence of the idea which is being imitated. The actual person or thing which is being imitated is elsewhere. The presence of the imitation, or rather the imitator, is here. This corresponds directly to the question of reality and truthfulness of mimesis, or presence. Aristotle clarifies this paradox in chapter 15 of his *Poetics*. He states that the initial imitation must be enhanced, embellished, and directed towards an ideal.

> The artist who gives form to raw material then works in a manner parallel to that of nature itself and, by observing the partially realized forms in nature, may anticipate their completion. In this way he shows things not as they are but as they "ought to be."[3]

In the *History of the Greek and Roman Theatre* Margarete Bieber states:

> [the] Dramatic art requires the actor to lay aside the personality with which he was endowed and to feel himself as one who has abandoned the limitations of his own personality. He must lose his own identity and become a changed being, a demon, a god, or a hero.[4]

These attitudes towards style, mimesis, and action were reflected in the bodily movements of the actors of the ancient Greek theatre. Although it is unfortunate that firsthand descriptions of the style of acting during this period do not exist, it is generally accepted that the movements and gestures of the actors were simple and broad, which denoted a refined and elegant style. Bieber says that the movements of the actors were affected by the costumes worn in that day. The actor lost his own identity as a result of being almost completely covered and made unrecognizable.[5] The movements of actors in comedy were different from those of tragedy, often with movements and postures ranging from the ordinary to the outrageous. "Voice and gesture had to fit the size of the theatre. One can expect strong and simple motions in tragedy and lively exaggerated motions in comedy. Running and violent gesticulation with the arm are the rule."[6]

Movement and gesture took on an accepted meaning as in mimetic dance. Greek dance, which was often a part of the dramatic theatre, was divided into the *emmeleia* and the *schemata,* or movements which were performed in order to display deep emotions. These schemata were recognized as a particular sequence of movements, such as the showing of grief by tearing the hair, or the grasping of knees to display supplication. Michael Walton in *The Greek Sense of Tragedy* equates these schemata with the five positions in classical ballet, in that each of the sequence of movements could be used in any combination to project a desired emotion or emotional state.[7]

The Greek theatre was a visual as well as an aural experience. The actor worked within a backdrop of music as well as dance, and while he was always aware that his performance was a kind of dance, the spoken word was the basis of the tragic form. Beauty of voice quality, ability to project emotional ranges, and adaptability of voice were of primary importance to the Greek actor.

> Since the representational art of the first century however, with few exceptions—the pediment figures from the temple of Zeus at Olympia, the wall paintings by Pistoxenus—did not express feelings and passions by the play of features, but rather through the posture and movements of the whole body. . . . [W]e may conclude that the art of acting in the 5th and in the following centuries also laid the greatest emphasis on these methods. In addition, the actor had not only to master the art of speaking, but he had to be able to declaim and sing to music. Singing and reciting were accompanied by the flute. . . . Clearness of voice and correct enunciation were more important that a strong voice, as the splendid acoustics in the Greek theatre let spoken word and song reach the uppermost rows.[8]

The fact that the Greek actors were masked represents a fundamental influence on the style of acting during the fifth century B.C. The language of the Greek theatre was one in which gesture or movement underscored the verbal or spoken image. The mask offered a unique dimension to the theatre.

> To start with the mask is not to confine Greek acting to it. It was a part of the actor's externals, as were any other aspects of his costume, though there is evidence that he regarded it as central to his performance. But the actor himself was only a part of the stage composite which related him to both background and foreground and attuned his physical aspect to the words he spoke and the situation in which his character was placed.[9]

Acting in a mask actually requires more attention given to the gestures, posture, and movement of the actor. The mask does convey a particular and static expression, but how the actor shows attention, for example, presents a particular problem. A problem which, for the Greek actor, meant that his acting required more "acting."

> Because the masked actor cannot rely only on his face to portray emotion, but must find a total physical expression to amplify his words, so the other members of a stage group cannot listen impassively without nullifying the statement of the speaker. In a mask impassivity is active, not passive. This is not to suggest that the person addressed need be as mobile as the speaker, but it does imply that at any moment within a performance of an Athenian tragedy the stage picture was composed of the physical postures of all present.[10]

As was common to the Greeks of the day, discipline, beauty, and form were goals of actor training. The training program for actors was long and difficult, and involved physical exercise as well as strenuous vocal work.

> Voice was the prime concern of every Greek tragedian because his gestures and movements were simple and restrained, because his facial expressions were concealed behind a mask, and because his huge theatre wasn't too much "a place for seeing."[11]

Edwin Duerr in *The Length and Depth of Acting* is consistent with the long held belief that the emphasis in the Greek theatre was on the spoken word, or the text rather than on the visual performance by the actor. Recent theories may suggest otherwise. According to the valuable work on ancient Greek dance by Lillian Lawler and views presented by Michael Walton in *The Greek Sense of Theatre*, the focus of the Greek theatre was on the actor and his ability to express emotion physically.

> [I]t is still the common belief that what was *said* in the Greek tragedies was more important that what was seen. It was not so. . . . The actor may have been *hupokrites*, an "answerer" or "expounder of a story," but the *chorus* was a chorus of dancers who performed in an orchestre, not a place for musicians as in English usage, but a dancing-place. The action of the play was a "drama," "something done," not "something spoken," and the spectators, *theatai,* sat, not in an auditorium, a "hearing place," but in a *theatron,* a "seeing-place." The Greeks went to the theatre to witness a performance.[12]

The Athenian theatre was a place of great visual detail, but because it is now impossible to recreate the movements and actual performance of a Greek tragedy in its original style, the emphasis inadvertently falls on the text. The characters of the Greek tragedy spoke through the entire language of the theatre — gesture, movement, dance, posture, and voice, intonation and text. It is suggested that the Greek theatre may have been more like a modern ballet or opera than a traditional theatrical production. Another parallel can be drawn between the Greek theatre and the modern work of Jerzy Grotowski and his Polish Lab Theatre in which text is subordinate to the physical essence of character. Both styles of theatre, one ancient and one modern, focus on simplicity, cathartic release, and audience involvement. Both require exact discipline and training.

We know little of the exact executions of drama in the ancient Greek world. We have the extant plays, the vase paintings, and the guidelines left by Aristotle. This is hardly enough. Experts agree that by the fifth and fourth centuries B.C. the actor had attained a level of professional status and that his dramatic actions were free and expressive. Not only did the actor of this time act and move expressively, he also had to sing and recite to music. The entire body became an expressive instrument.

The Greeks believed in an ideal form of beauty. This ideal included beauty as it related to art, architecture, literature, music, and the human form. The ideal beauty of the human form could be achieved through constant physical training. The strength, grace, and suppleness which resulted were evidenced by actors on the stage. The Greek costume was an extension of the beautiful form — the fabric hung in fluid drapes on the body and revealed the human form in long, elegant lines.

The physical actions of the plays rarely call for characters to sit. Actions include kneeling, walking, carrying out sacrificial duties, exhibiting intense emotions (anger, grief, madness, and passion), and limited physical contact with other characters.

The Greeks heightened their language and we are left with tragic, moving plays. Unfortunately, what we can only imagine is the sight of the actors as they danced their grief, physically expressed their all-consuming hate, or moved their way into the throes of wanton passion.

The visual sense is lost to us. However little we can be sure of in Greek acting and movement, it does seem apparent that there existed a strong sense of going beyond realism as we would define it today. They approached a kind of theatricalization of movement: an abstraction, so that a higher level of emotion and character could be communicated. The theatre was probably a prime example of the level of balance the Greeks achieved in their art.

3. The Romans:
Oratory and Entertainment

That the Romans borrowed much from the Greeks is especially evident in their sculpture, theatre, plays, and architecture. What the Romans did not have to borrow or imitate from their Greek predecessors was the natural gift and talent for acting. The Romans had a certain skill in the use of language and were known for their lively and animated movements and gestures. Improvisation, mime, and acting were natural expressions of these attributes. The major contribution to the art of acting was the Roman attitude toward actor training.

The Roman actor was subjected to strict training, like that of an athlete. The voice and body were molded into a finely tuned instrument capable of expressing attitudes and gestures that exactly corresponded to the spoken word or music.

Facial expression became an important dramatic tool in the Roman theatre because unlike the Greeks, Roman mime used no masks.

By the first century B.C. the idea of theatre changed radically from its classical beginnings hundreds of years before in Greece. Theatre was no longer a religious ritual associated with religious festivals. By the first century A.D. theatre was more often associated with pagan ceremonies and rituals. Another change which occurred was the variety of types of theatrical performances. The Roman theatre was a theatre of entertainment which included mime plays, coarse farces, solemn tragedies (usually based on Greek themes), and bawdy comedies. For each type of performance there were different costumes as well as different movements and gestures. Comedies were lively, quick, and active.

17

Tragedies were sober, slow, and elegant. Farces were often lewd, obscene (by modern standards), and ridiculous.

The actor's approach to acting was delineated along specific codes of appropriate movement, gesture, action and, where applicable, facial expression. However, the attitude toward the intellectual or emotional connection with the character was changing. Since the actor no longer had the idea of the *presence* of spirit from which to inspire him he now began to focus on a more rational, planned approach to acting.

The great Roman orator Quintilian (A.D. 35–95) posed a question which can be traced back to Aristotle and Horace and which has continued to plague aestheticians through to today. "If we are to stir emotions in others by first feeling them ourselves, how do we generate these emotions in ourselves?"

> An orator, . . . like an actor, should employ imaginative identification to "impersonate" and "exhibit" emotions as if they were his own. He urges the orator to "assimilate [himself] to the emotions of those who are genuinely so affected," taking those passions into himself and transforming them into vocal and bodily eloquence.[1]

Although the Romans differed from the Greeks in many ways, their plays as well as their acting styles were modeled after the Greeks. Rome had its native drama but most plays were translations from the Greek. The most significant difference was in the entertainment quality of the performances and the actors. Often the plays were accompanied by chariot races, gladiator shows, and mock war scenes. Most actors were slaves who fell at the mercy of an entertainment-hungry audience. Roman actors excelled in their exuberance and virtuosity. Acting during the Roman times was characterized by pantomimic gesturing and detailed use of the hands. In training, emphasis was also on the voice.

Quintilian focuses on the use of *pathos* to evoke a response from the audience. The Greeks considered this principle, yet Quintilian pursued it one step further. He suggested that the actor (or the orator) feel the emotions as though they were his own. Suddenly the actor was no longer imitating but exhibiting and internalizing feelings to the point of impersonation. Livius Andronicus (240 B.C.), a captive Greek, was instrumental in focusing attention on movement and gesture by separating the actor's actions from his speech. The Greek Aesop was well known for his emotional performances as well as the extent of his pantomimic talent. Yet the Romans, like their Greek predecessors, faced the fundamental question: "If passions and emotions were strongly felt in the body, why not allow the body to express such emotions?"

> Apollo, it was thought, took the form of intoxicating vapors and breathed himself into the mouth or other convenient orifice of the Pythoness of Delphi as she squatted astride the divine tripod; the "Spirit" which then lived in her and spake through her, moving her lips "as long as she was in frenzy," was the oracular god Himself. In Quintilian's time these supernatural manifestations were thought to be inherent in the nature of the body itself. The *praecordia* or diaphragm was viewed as a barometer of the passions; and the association of breath, thought, and blood explained the characteristic physiological manifestations of strong emotion including the heaving breast, blushing, bulging veins in the neck, choking, and purpling with rage, and sighing with grief.[2]

The Romans questioned the nature of dramatic acting. No longer accepting the "spiritual" answer, as did the Greeks, they looked to the organic cause and effect of emotion. The obsession for scientific knowledge of the human body persisted throughout the medieval and Renaissance periods.

An additional influence on the attitudes toward stage movement was the mime, or *fabula ricinata*. First appearing in Rome in 211 B.C. it grew into a short, but often elaborate, theatrical form. Unusually comic, it focused on events of everyday life and employed scenes of violent and obscene action. These mimes bridged the gap between acting and the actor's movements and what would later develop into a distinct dance form. Lucian (A.D. 120–200) is the author of the most famous writing on pantomime of this period. He is careful to suggest that the mime depends, as does the actor, on verisimilitude.

> The fact is, the pantomime must be completely armed at every point. His work must be one harmonious whole, perfect in balance and proportion, self-consistent. . . .
>
> But in Pantomime, as in rhetoric, there can be (to use a popular phrase) too much of a good thing; a man may exceed the proper bounds of imitation. . . .[3]

The actors of second century Rome most assuredly were a different breed of actor than their Greek counterparts. Often called upon for other types of entertainment, their feats ranged from juggling and acrobatics, to dancing. It appears that styles of acting fitted the type of dramatic form: tragedy, comedy, mime, or pantomime (*fabula saltica*).

The predominate use of stock actions seems well accepted in this period. These actions probably included gestures, poses, attitudes, and movement patterns which were symbolic and evocative of specific emotional or comic states.

> The art of acting was highly developed among the Romans. The Italian natives have always had a special gift for mimicry. They are born improvisators, having lively gestures and great skill in the use of language. To this was added in Roman times a strict training which is described by Cicero. He says that the actor needs the physical training of an athlete and of a dancer. Quintilian recommends to public speakers that they imitate the art of the actors for their gestures.[4]

Roman actors and mimes, like their Greek counterparts, took everyday actions and gestures and then stylized and conventionalized them for theatrical effect.

Finally, major differences between the Greek and Roman physical theatre had a profound effect, however indirectly, on the style of movement and especially on the relationship between actor and audience. The major acting area in the Greek theatre (the orchestra) was a full circle which was high and shallow. The Roman orchestra is a half circle and is low and deep. The Greek theatres, traditionally built in the side of a mountain and often with a southern exposure, were religious buildings in which all patrons had equally good seats. The Romans, on the other hand, built their theatres on level ground and had different seats for the different levels of society. The Romans provided a place for the modern idea of a theatre as a whole, including a connecting station for scenic background, the stage house, the orchestra, and stage entrances.

The influence of the actor's art throughout the medieval period was centered on the following premises:

> First, the actor possessed the power to act on his own body. Second, he possessed the power to act on the physical space around him. Finally, he was able to act on the bodies of the spectators who shared that space with him. In short, he possessed the power to act. His expressions could

transfer his physical identity, inwardly and outwardly and so thoroughly that at his best he was known as Proteus.[5]

Surely actors had accomplished a giant leap forward in terms of acceptance and focus on the body as the center of character personification. Yet it was this interest in the body, this semiscientific adherence to rules of body movement, which persisted for almost two thousand years. If movements and their emotional results could be calculated both in the actor and the onlooker, then precise rules of movement could be prescribed for the actor.

With the decline of the Roman Empire, theatre, like science, literature, and technology, slipped into the Dark Ages. Traveling troupes, wandering mimes, and animal trainers exhibited their talents from town to village. In the fourteenth and fifteenth centuries the actor was resurrected to perform Biblical narratives. The professional actor outside the realm of the Church did not resurface until well into the sixteenth century. The Elizabethan period saw the restoration of professional acting combined with playwrighting in its highest form. The English Renaissance was a time of extraordinary innovation not only in writing, but in investigation of the world as well.

4. The Sixteenth and Seventeenth Centuries: Elizabethan and Rhetorical

The Roman desire for entertainment grew into a passion for wild and bloody games during the second and third centuries A.D. Comedies and tragedies were combined with or replaced by mock naval battles, gladiator battles, and wild animal shows. By the time slaves and prisoners of war were replaced by Christians as victims in some of the bloody sports, the end of Roman theatre was near.

Christianity was gaining acceptance in the fifth century A.D. and it was no longer unlawful to proclaim oneself a Christian. Thereafter, the arenas and theatres were closed because they were associated with pagan rituals and ceremonies, which were considered immoral, and theatrical performances usually ridiculed Christians and their practices. Theatre as a public and entertainment institution ceased to exist for at least the next seven hundred years. However, this did not mean that theatrical performances ceased. On the contrary, scores of minstrels, jugglers, mimes, jesters, and traveling players continued to perform in small towns and villages. These lower class performances took the place of the classical literary drama. They performed in courtyards, inns, and castles, and then moved on to the next village. Theatre was forced, once again, to seek its ritual roots. After lying dormant for centuries it found them in the Church.

Since most of the performances during the Middle Ages were performed by individuals or small groups, there was not a common accepted style of acting or movement. The key during this period was adaptability. Since shows traveled from place to place each actor or performer had to continually rely on his own talents. It does seem that actors had to have great agility and command of their bodies in order to maintain an audience. Acrobatic skills, juggling, rope dancing, and a quick mind (for memorizing ballads, poems, folktales, and scenarios) were vital to the actor. Knowledge of folk dances, couple dancing, and choral dancing also was important.

Theatre as ritual had its second rebirth in the mass and the hours service in the Church. These ritual performances were complete with chants, processions, and oral stories. Although these early Church services were not performed by actors but by priests, they were considered rituals since they were performed precisely in accord with tradition and for the attainment of some desired end. As these services became more complex and it became increasingly important to involve and inspire the predominately illiterate congregation, the enactment of biblical stories moved outside the Church into the courtyard or town square. Biblical drama, including mystery and morality plays, became popular. The movement from inside the Church to the outside courtyard represented a significant change not only in the types of drama but in the performers of the drama. The plays performed outside the Church eventually took on a less biblical theme (that is, no longer were biblical characters the sole focus). Common mortals in their struggle against evil became the central characters. The professional actor began to replace the priest and Church layperson.

By the fifteenth century the works of Plautus and Terence were still being performed. This provided further evidence that theatre was moving, once again, away from the ritual connection to the arena of entertainment. In the sixteenth century the Roman comedies of Plautus and Terence were performed in Spain, Germany, and Holland. The Elizabethans were fond of Plautus and Terence and it is certain that Shakespeare was familiar with these classic comedies. The influence of Seneca's tragedies is also evident in many Elizabethan dramas including those of Shakespeare.

Major changes in the style of acting occurred in the Elizabethan period. Codes of movement and behavior were established and high standards in the quality of acting were observed. The Elizabethan actor took on a special attitude towards decorum, or the dignity of behavior. The actor must appear graceful, elegant, poised, and stylized. The ideal for the Elizabethan actor is described by Shakespeare's Hamlet in his speech to the players.

The Elizabethan actor was, both in voice and gesture, well within the bounds of decorum. The prime focus in training, it is true, was on the voice. Movement was somewhat formal and stylized, but with realistic gestures and mannerisms. In terms of movement training the Elizabethan actor was expected to be able to fence, dance, and move with grace. Comedy often included tumbling and leaping. The actor's courtly appearance both in dancing and fencing was necessary to the elegance and excitement of tragedy.

Although Elizabethan acting was more realistic than that of the Greeks or Romans, an element of stylization was necessary partly because of the fact that women still did not appear on stage. Young men played female roles like those of Lady Macbeth or Juliet. In order for their performances to appear realistic they must also be stylized. If the female characters on stage were performed with stylization the male characters had to be played similarly, to maintain a consistency of the whole performance.

The theatre art of the seventeenth century embodied the rhetorical and oratorical styles which had been passed down from as far back as Quintilian. It was, in fact, Quintilian who prescribed "...never ... employ the left hand alone in gesture; [and] ... the art of gesture will not permit the hand to be raised above the level of the eyes...."[1]

The relationship between costume and movement was an important one during this period because the construction and physical restrictions of the costume often determined the type of movement which could be executed by the actor. The changes in movement styles from the fifteenth to the seventeenth century were, in part, brought about because of changes in the costume styles. The costumes became more rigid and stiff as the seventeenth century approached. Movements for men became increasingly swaggering because of the stiffening and padding used around the arms and thighs. The Spanish farthingale presented particular restrictions on women's movements, especially sitting and curtseying.

Rules of stage behavior and presentation followed the strict standards of decorum of that time. This system of rhetorical acting seems most inhibiting and constrained to those of us in the twentieth century,

yet it embodied a way of thinking which was most reflective and percep-
tive of the age. It was during the seventeenth century that the influence
of ancient medicine and the scientific revolution was first apparent.

> To the extent that modern critics and historians have lost sight
> of the scientific and pseudo-scientific underpinnings of rhetorical
> theory, our understanding of seventeenth-century actors and acting
> has been diminished. In consequence, a number of the tantalizingly
> meager accounts of contemporary performances seem even less de-
> scriptive and substantial than they are in fact. In 1612, for instance,
> when Thomas Heywood wrote of the "perfect shape to which [an
> actor] fashioned all his active spirits," he could assume his reader's
> comprehension of the Renaissance version of Galen's nerve physi-
> ology and its explanation of how those thoughts become action — just
> as an author on theatrical subjects today can safely assume the in-
> telligibility of a reference to conditioned reflexes.... The tiresome
> debate over the relative formalism or naturalism of seventeenth-
> century acting style can be traced to the disinclination of both sides
> to understand the historic link between acting, rhetoric, and ancient
> physiological doctrines. The same misunderstandings have been carried
> over into the study of acting in the Restoration period, the theory
> of which was no less rhetorically attuned and the popular physiological
> assumptions no less archaic. The rhetorical theory on which seventeenth-
> century discussions of acting were based rested on how the passions
> operate on the human body, specifically on the body of one who is
> actively transforming himself, "fashion[ing] all his active spirits," into
> some shape he has imagined.[2]

An overview of the acting styles of the seventeenth century does not
present a picture of realism, at least not as it would be defined by twentieth century terms. Acting in the 1600s was not naturally imitative of
real life. Decorum dictated a kind of elevated posture, eloquence in
movement and gesture, and a highly refined and restrained manner of
reflecting emotions or passions. It is important to understand, however,
that this style of movement was closely related to the scientific
knowledge of the day which connected the mind and body and how
they fit into the scheme of decorum and adherence to verisimilitude.

There was a sense of stability in the rhetorical style of acting of the
seventeenth century and a security in the acceptance that as long as one
were true to the laws of art a desired outcome could be achieved. For
example, it was believed that if an actor felt the passions of his role, and

he was technically proficient in verbally and physically acting the role, the same passions or effects of the passion would be passed on to the audience. The restrained movements and modulation of vocal tone kept the actor well within the bounds of acceptable decorum and the performance was believable to the onlookers. Those in the audience also accepted the application of certain rigid rules of behavior on the stage. Acting seemed simple, a technical feat which could be learned, mastered and performed.

The results of the scientific revolution were being felt by the end of the seventeenth century and consequently the world view was changing as well. At the center of much of the changes of this time was the theatre, a place where new trends and ideas were introduced and old ways were challenged. The time of rhetorical acting was growing short and a new style of acting, as well as aesthetic theory, was developing. This new style of acting was most evident in the performances of the British actor David Garrick. A French philosopher, Denis Diderot, also worked during this time and his contributions to theatrical theory, in general, were the most significant to this date.

5. The Eighteenth Century: Garrick and Diderot

David Garrick (1717–1779) was the epitome of successful acting during the eighteenth century. He was considered the "modern" actor of his day, the first to break with the rhetorical tradition and introduce audiences to his agile, varied, and energetic style. He broke with the past in "what historians of science would term a revolutionary paradigm shift."[1] To say that Garrick's style of acting was realistic is not altogether correct, especially when we understand the term "realistic acting" from a late twentieth century point of view. His style was based on observances of everyday life, though probably with an idealized attitude toward actions and vocal tones. Garrick's style of acting did represent a drastic change in attitudes toward acting and, especially, stage movement.

During the seventeenth century the primary emphasis of movement was on the actor's arms, hands, and fingers. A commonly accepted rule of the day was that of Quintilian never to gesture with the left hand alone (as quoted a few pages back). These rules of movement and manners were based on practices common to prosperous society and were published in books and letters during the period. Dancing masters were often hired so that fashionable young ladies and gentlemen were properly trained in the physical graces. Such graces included sitting and standing, walking and bowing, and handling accessories like hats, coats, fans, and purses.

The influence of the five basic positions of ballet (first used by Louis XIV of France in the late 1600s) was evident in the graceful, controlled

movements of both men and women. The head was carried erect,
shoulders held high, and the chest expanded upward. The feet were
turned out thus giving the body more light balance and an aesthetically
pleasing line to the leg.

Garrick and many of his contemporaries abandoned these rules and
began to employ the use of the total body in a more unrestrained and
natural manner. According to Garrick,

> Acting is an entertainment of the stage, which by calling in the aid and
> assistance of articulation, corporeal motion, and ocular expression, im-
> itates, assumes, or puts on the various mental and bodily emotions aris-
> ing from the various humors, virtues, and vices, incidents to human
> nature.[2]

Garrick also spoke of the body as a "moving statue" and this is ex-
emplary of what historians have described as his "posturing." Garrick
made an attempt to describe a more realistic style of acting and moving
on the stage. Although Garrick and his followers did move toward
greater realism during this time, some acting conventions remained the
same. Because stage scenery existed only as a backdrop the acting took
place on the downstage portion of the stage space. This forced the actor
to always face the audience. In addition, there was little or no stage fur-
nishings so much of the acting took place in a standing position. It was
a common practice for the audience to applaud after a key moment in
the actor's dramatic performance. This encouraged the actor to exag-
gerate and emphasize those passages. It is difficult for modern readers
to comprehend this style as being realistic based on Western experience
in the past fifty to eighty years.

> Today we tend to use *natural* and *organic* as synonyms. But in Garrick's
> day Romanticism, Naturalism, and Darwinism had yet to proclaim that
> we have more in common with the scum on the pond than with the
> statue in the park. In this respect we are the intellectual heirs of
> nineteenth-century science and its invention of the concept of biology,
> and when we try to gauge the ramifications of eighteenth-century scien-
> tific thought on theatrical practice and theory, we can do no better than
> heed Michel Foucault's warning that our own "pattern of knowledge" is
> simply "not valid" for that period.[3]

The fascinating element of Garrick's contribution to the field of
acting and stage movement, at least for twentieth century readers, is

that he laid the groundwork for theories and questions which still concern us today. He was the first to begin to contemplate those concepts within the field of scientific knowledge that Stanislavski, Artaud, and Grotowski were to question later. Garrick pioneered the use of more rehearsal time. He encouraged actors to listen to one another on stage — to actually listen and to look at one another as though they were listening. This important transition broke the actor from the idea that he was reciting his lines. As actors began to interact with one another on stage they also began to interpret their lines from an individualized standpoint. Garrick emphasized that actors should act realistically, not symbolically.

The acting of Garrick's day represented a relationship, if not a struggle, between the plastic arts and theatrical theory. This relationship corresponds naturally to the accepted eighteenth century definition of action, which was ". . . the alternation between periods of action and moments of static tableaux."[4]

Movement became an important element in the acting of the day because it represented a synthesis of mind, body, psyche, and temperament at a given moment in the life of the character.

By the end of the eighteenth century the questions which persisted in the minds of theatre theorists concerned how the responsive body could best embody emotion and still remain believable and acceptable. Medieval and physical sciences aided in the wealth of information, as did the philosophical theories accumulated to the day. "The task would be left to Diderot, the theorist, who . . . foresaw the main innovation of nineteenth century science, the development of life as a mental category."[5]

Denis Diderot (1713–1784) was a man in search of knowledge. He was fascinated by how things were put together and how things worked. His quest for answers to these questions led him to study science, medicine, and mechanical power, as well as the fine arts. In the many volumes of his complete works he explored a full range of subjects from the making of windmills or the operation of knitting machines, to the use of surgical instruments and choreographic notation. Perhaps he is remembered best for his theories raised in the 1773 work *The Paradox of Acting,* which explores the basic elements of acting.

> To this day many acting theorists, knowingly or unknowingly, formulate their views in response to perspectives introduced in the *Paradoxe*. Foremost among them is the stand on the notorious question of emotionality. Like John Hill, the Riccobonies, Lessing, and Sainte-Albine, Diderot asked himself if the actor should sincerely feel the passions he portrays onstage. Unlike their answers, however, Diderot's firm negative had the power to revolutionize acting theory....[6]

Diderot's revolution was founded on the premise that the actor should do away with extreme sensibility. It made for "muddling actors"[7] and without it, actors had the possibility of greatness. In his essays Diderot takes an early look at such concepts as emotion memory, ensemble playing, concentration, public solitude, spontaneity, and imagination, although he was not responsible for the titles which we associate with these concepts in the twentieth century.

Diderot's approach to acting was as a craft, not some Apollonian spirit which surrounded the actor and attached him from without. Rather, Diderot believed that the actor was in control of what he felt, what he understood, and what he projected. Diderot reversed himself many times and continually was drawn back to the question of mimesis, imitation and the real presence of the character through the actor. He finally concluded that true mimesis (imitation) does not occur. What does occur, in fact, is a selective process by which the actor chooses certain moments or reflections of reality which are calculated carefully to obtain a desired result. To accomplish this illusion Diderot suggested the use of a strong and vivid imagination which could be combined with a responsive and agile body. Diderot also believed in exact duplication. He accepted the possibility of an actor's being able to perform his or her role in the same manner with passionate intensity or quiet contemplation, over and over again. To imply that this type of acting was mechanical misses the point. It was as though Diderot instructed a model or inner characterization which could dictate the performance at any time, or many times over.

Diderot was a genius and he was a man of his times. His revolutionary theories on acting affected subsequent ways of thinking not only about acting but the style and process as well. Though he did accept a new kind of suggested realism, Diderot also accepted that the movements of the actor must be magnified for the stage. Gestures must be broad, facial expressions must be visible, and the voice must be loud and articulate.

Diderot was eager to acknowledge that stage movement was, or should be, quite different from reality. But he was opposed to the idea that "Actors remain equidistant in artificial semicircles," never daring "to look each other in the face, turn their backs to the spectator, move close to one another, part or rejoin."[8] He was an advocate of natural movements which could be executed in an easy and fluid manner. He once suggested that the actor look at the groupings in paintings for informal arrangements which were more pleasing to the eye.

In terms of the creative process, Diderot accounts for three steps of creation for the actor in search of his role. He outlines the first as *observation*. (This is not unlike the steps outlined by Stanislavski some one hundred and seventy years later.) Observation of passions, bodily movements, and physical responses comprises the actor's first step in character development. These reactions, whether physical or emotional, were subject to stage decorum, as well as morally acceptable expressions of the day.

The second stage consists of a *reflection*. At this point the actor reflects on his observations from real life. Combining his memory (reflection) with his imagination he can formulate a clear matrix, or core of the character. This reflective stage draws on conscious as well as subconscious impression. By this point the actor has a clear picture of the gestures, bodily movements, attitudes, and vocal intonation which would be proper for the role.

In the third stage the actor *experiments*. The role is perfected and duplicated through exhaustive experimentation which employs the imaginative and reflective powers. The matrix or inner model of the character serves as a direction for the ideal manner of performance. Once this model is perfected the performance of the character can be duplicated many times over.

> After exhausting the range of choices open to him, the actor will have created the inner model, which serves as the matrix for all his subsequent performances of that role. This explains to Diderot's satisfaction the several reasons why great actors perform consistently from day to day: nothing is left to the inspiration of the moment; the blueprint remains before their mind's eye, guiding each step and each utterance

onstage; it promotes a uniformity of muscular motion, carefully built up
bit by bit during rehearsal, comparable to the fusing of reflex and habit
in the creation of a gymnastic routine....[9]

Diderot was fascinated with the actor and the physical interpreta-
tion of a role. He placed an almost obsessive interest on the body and
its capacity to project character. In 1751 in his *Lettre sur les sourds et
muets,* Diderot recalls sitting in the theatre with his fingers in his ears.
In his attempt to eliminate all sounds coming from the stage, he was
made aware of the overwhelming impact of the actor's body. He found
that a great actor could project much more than thought possible
through the use of face and body. The actor, he thought, should train
like the pianist or the ballet dancer in order to get the passion or the
intensity into the muscles and into the kinesthetic "muscle memory."

Diderot's legacy evolved into more than an attack on or an
adherence to this theory of acting. Surely, in today's aesthetic discus-
sions he is the one most challenged, if not the most revered, of theorists.
Yet he has left us a greater body of knowledge than what was outlined
in *The Paradox of Acting.* Diderot spoke of those things which bridged
the gap between the scientific, physiological world of his day, and the
concepts of what theatre art should be and has become. His idea of
character model changed the process of acting as well as the performance. What twentieth century acting theorists call by such names as
psychological gesture, core character, or given circumstances, can be
traced back to the concepts first investigated by Diderot. The exhaustive
and lengthy rehearsal schedules dictated by Diderot were later emulated
by the Moscow Art Theatre and the Duke of Saxe-Meinigen. Brecht,
Meyerhold, and the Futurists have a debt to pay to Diderot for his work
in the mechanics of the actor.

Diderot advanced the theories of acting and consequently changed
the existing attitudes toward the actor's body, its uses, its training, and
its power in performance. Because of Diderot, stage movement emerged
as a vital ingredient in theatre performance, one which must be trained,
perfected, and given its rightful place in the craft of acting.

As Diderot specifically anticipated, the lines of modern theatrical argu-
ment paralleled and overlapped the historic contention between

biological vitalists and mechanists, a collision and at times a confusion of viewpoints that had more complicated implications that those increasingly obsolete terms could depict. At root the question came down to this: Is the actor's bodily instrument to be interpreted as a spontaneously vital organism whose innate powers of feeling must somehow naturally predominate? Or is it best understood as a biological machine, structured by and reducible to so many physical and chemical processes, whose receptivity to reflex conditioning determines its behavior?[10]

During the nineteenth century the issue of mind-and-body became an accepted principle. Not only were the mind and body inexorably connected but they served together in a continuum, rather than a duality. This acceptance of scientific theory was a springboard to the twentieth century works of Meyerhold, Stanislavski, Grotowski, and the avant-garde theorists of the 1960s and 1970s and later. But first a nineteenth century actor and professor made another important contribution in the area of stage movement. His name was François Delsarte.

6. Subjective Idealism: Romanticism and Delsarte

The Romantic era brought to an end a way of thinking which had existed since the early Renaissance. Rationalism and the ideals of the Enlightenment withered under the oppression of the Napoleonic period. Life was changing. Industrialism was on its way and with it came a change in the agrarian pattern of poor versus rich. The transitions of this time placed a strain on nearly everyone.

Poets, painters, and playwrights reacted to feelings of alienation towards the new industrialism by escaping into exotic fantasy or emotional sentimentality. The true romantic could be defined through an understanding of the word *sublime*. The sublime represented the unleashed beauty of nature — untamed and unrestricted. Examples include paintings of great storms and magnificent seascapes, emotionally intense music, and works of art which praised and glorified nature — the beautiful as well as the grotesque and the ugly. If one transferred this same idea into dramatic character the result is powerful human emotions which cannot be contained or restrained by reason. Characterization was second to feeling. Specifically the actor's movements were larger then life. Gestures and mannerisms were expansive, extending out and away from the body. The movements of the actor were completed in sweeping curves to emphasize their grandeur and scope. This was reemphasized through the type of costumes worn in the early nineteenth century. It must be noted, however that the stage movements of the Romantic period were more relaxed than those of the seventeenth and eighteenth centuries.

At the same time that actors were fascinated with all facets of the expression of emotion they began to combine scientific and sometimes medical knowledge with their theatre training. There continued to be a mystery which surrounded the wellspring from which emotion erupted. The writings of Darwin along with current scientific thought offered a key to solving this mystery. If emotion could be measured through movement—facial expression, gesture, posture, and mannerisms—then it seemed possible that emotion could be evoked through the execution of certain movement codes. It was this theory which led François Delsarte to his method of acting and actor training.

The accounts of the early life of movement theorist Delsarte are vague and in some cases contradictory. Much of the information is legend or speculation. But history does confirm that he was born François Alexandre Nicolas Chéri Delsarte (1811–1871) in Solesmes, France. He apprenticed as a painter for a time and was soon taken in by Pere Bambini to develop his musical talents. In 1825 he entered the Conservatoire in Paris and a promising career seemed certain. It was during his education at the Conservatoire that he first encountered stage movement and stage diction as part of his course of study. The following account demonstrates the varied opinions of the day towards proper stage speech and movement.

> On one account Delsarte attempted to recite a series of verses to four different professors on four successive days. Professor Number One recommended that the "express those lines with amplitude, with dignity, with nobleness." After assiduous practice, Delsarte brought his "noble" delivery to Professor Number Two. His efforts produced a "formidable burst of laughter, followed by the advice that the "lines should be said naturally, simply, and with all possible *bonhommie*." After careful rehearsal according to the dictates of the second instructor, he presented his efforts to Number Three. He was allowed to utter fewer than four words before being called an idiot and given a fresh, and, of course, contradictory, set of suggestions. On the following day his experience with Number Four was no more successful.
>
> Both vocal interpretations and physical expressions came under the scrutiny of these instructors. These men seemed unable to provide valid counsel in either area.[1]

Understandably, Delsarte became frustrated with his training at the Conservatoire and with his lack of guidance, especially in the areas of movement and gesture. It was this feeling of frustration which prompted him to begin to develop a "system" for the training of the actor's body. In 1830 he left the Conservatoire and, as fate would have it, began to experience problems with his voice. Perhaps the deterioration was a result of poor training (Delsarte blamed his poor instruction for the loss of his voice), or it is possible his problems were physiological. In any case this setback ultimately proved a gift in disguise, for he literally had no alternative but to experiment, explore, and develop a new "system" for the training and use of the actor's physical expression.

Delsarte attempted to develop scientific-like rules, or laws, to which the voice and body of the actor could be subjected. He was dissatisfied with the training methods of that time and sought to instruct actors in stage movements which were more natural and acceptable. By 1839 he was ready to begin his instruction. He was widely accepted in the United States and was responsible for the success of a number of distinguished pupils, among them, American-born James Steele MacKaye. It was through the writings and encouragement of MacKaye that Delsarte's work became so widely accepted and so popular in the United States.

Delsarte continued, through failing health, to write and document his theories up until 1870. At that point much of his work was either left unfinished or was taken up by a number of his pupils. Unfortunately, only a small portion of the planned works of Delsarte's system were completed, and, like so many theorists, his writings were and are subject to grave misinterpretation.

Delsarte wrote that "The artist should have three objects: To *move*, to *interest*, to *persuade*. He interests by *language;* he moves by *thought;* he moves, interests, and persuades by *gesture.*"[2] Delsarte was especially interested in gesture and the power of movement. It must be noted that Delsarte was a deeply religious man who held his religious convictions almost to the point of obsession. He considered his work divinely inspired and grouped many of his theories in threes in accordance with the Holy Trinity. He divided the body into three zones; the chest for mental activity, the heart for moral activity, and the abdomen for organic activity. Each zone denoted certain types of movements or gestures and could evoke specific emotional responses from the onlooker. He attempted to delve into the "inner" actor and connect body movements

with emotional or thinking stimuli. Ultimately, he arrived at an in-
credibly elaborate system whereby each part of the body was positioned
for certain emotional levels. The system was later thought to be too
mechanistic, too rigid. Yet by the end of the nineteenth century his
system was being taught all over the world.

> Delsarte, reacting against the mechanical and formalized actor training
> of his time, attempted to return to nature by carefully observing and
> recording those expressions and gestures produced not by art but by in-
> stinct and emotion. But when these were codified for his students, the
> result was yet another mechanical system, the formal details of which
> were so rigorously taught by Delsarte's disciples for the remainder of the
> century that even today his system is almost a synonym for mechanical,
> arbitrary expressions and gestures, the very thing it was created to
> prevent.[3]

By the end of the nineteenth century numerous texts were written
about Delsarte and his system.

> Most of the texts contain extremely simplified versions of Delsarte's
> system. Many are no more than collections of recitations, with sugges-
> tions for appropriate movements on specific passages. A few carry ver-
> sions of the ninefold accord, but rarely do they indicate the complexity
> of its potential application. Rather, they promote the popular concept
> that Delsarte envisioned nine positions for each part of the body, posi-
> tions which the actor can quickly assimilate to achieve correct gestures
> in any context. In general, they give the impression that the Delsarte
> system is simple, arbitrary and artificial.[4]

Delsarte had the right idea, but he was out of step with time. Perhaps
if his theories of movement and gesture could have been combined with
the early twentieth century principles of psychology they might have
grown into a less rigid manner of performance.

By the 1890s Delsarte's original concept of a movement system
which would free the actor to become more natural and realistic had
been diluted into a commerical advertising gimmick as well as an "in
vogue" art form for young ladies of stylish upbringings. The poses advocated by Delsarte were associated with bust girdles, fruited soaps, and
even a wooden leg. Young ladies donned Greek-style dress and spent
evenings entertaining invited guests to an "artistic statue posing." As

history is written, however, Delsarte's contributions were in the area of actor training. His style of acting is now judged as antiquated and unrealistic.

By the close of the nineteenth century new changes were again in the wind, changes which so dramatically affected all aspects of theatre that the results are still being calculated today. During the last quarter of the nineteenth century the demand was for greater realism and verisimilitude in speech, movement, and language. The plays of the new realists such as Ibsen, Strindberg, and Hauptmann, gave actors a new opportunity to experience and perform characters who spoke in a realistic fashion and who lived in life-like and sometimes unsavory circumstances. This trend, of course, called for a new style of movement for the actor, a new emphasis on stage movement, gesture, and characterization.

If the history of acting were told through the movements of the actor it would be a changing scenario. Each age had its own model through which the actor told his story. At first he was masked in ritual spiritualism. The spirit was the actor and in that sense his movements were not his own. He was oracle, a dancing, chanting presence. The questioning nature of man sought a different direction. The mask was dropped and the actor emerged as entertainer, no longer connected with the religious roots which gave rise to the drama.

As the actor changed so did his movements, and more importantly, his vision of his world and his explanation of it. Upon a closer inspection of the history of acting it is the movements of the actor which reveal the true nature of the art. Sometimes reflecting human acceptance of control, and sometimes rebelling against it, the actor was a unique barometer, in effect explaining many things through his or her art.

Where do emotions come from? How, if at all, can they be controlled? What is the relationship of art to life? And finally, does the recreation of emotion link us to some ancient, primitive calling deep within us? Each age struggled to answer these questions. Those struggles are most evident in the external workings of the actor. The physical manifestations of the actor are evident whether he or she creates from behind a mask, truly feels the emotion, or merely imposes a choreographed movement to fit the text. The actor moves, and the text will always be subordinate.

7. The Early Twentieth Century: Constantin Stanislavski

The twentieth century is an age of innovation. An age of great hope combined with periods of extreme despair, it has served as witness to the ultimate capacity of man. No other period in history has been so diverse, so complex, and so inventive. The writings of Darwin first published in the 1860s gave us a glimpse of our origins. To some, this view was shattering. That man was somehow connected with the animals, not only in ancestry but in the ultimate idea of creation, was not a comfortable thought for them.

Freud began writing in the 1880s and we have defined ourselves quite differently since then. If Darwin suggested we came from animals, Freud implied that we were animals. World War I proved that we were capable of acting as animals. Human inhumanity was, by 1915, proven. Survival of the fittest was interpreted in human destructive power.

Questions concerning man's ultimate nature were threatened with a new power—the machine. The Industrial Revolution, begun in the nineteenth century, stripped humans of their high place in the order of things. In many ways the machine was more powerful. A human creator-god made the machine, but like the biblical original man and woman, the machine was a renegade. Finally, family and societal traditions were altered through the rise of the women's movement. The family structure and the roles of men and women were not spared. As women moved out of the home and into the workplace new roles were created.

Out of these changes grew a time of great questioning. Nowhere was this more evident than in the theatre. The plays, the production shows, acting methods and techniques, and the advent of film reflected man's search for peace, understanding, and a sense of "who am I?"

Three leaders in the theatre of the twentieth century were Vsevolod Meyerhold, Constantin Stanislavski, and Jerzy Grotowski. They embodied this age in their quest for a true art of the twentieth century. Each man had a great respect for and interest in the theories and practices of the past. Each took his own direction in pursuing that art. Each of these three artists was connected in some way to one another and to the theatre of the past. In a review of their writings each often refers to past practitioners. Stanislavski pondered the same questions as Diderot. Meyerhold was influenced by the Greeks, the traditions of *commedia,* and by Stanislavski. Grotowski was a follower of Stanislavski, and Meyerhold, of the Greeks and Oriental theatre, as well as the avant-garde leader Antonin Artaud.

Each of these three men had special interest in the movement and external characterizations of the actor. Stanislavski, Meyerhold, and Grotowski knew that the actor was an expressive creature, especially in his movement expressions. Much of their focus in acting was directed towards the movement training and movement expression of the actor.

Perhaps the most important theatrical personality of the late nineteenth and early twentieth centuries was Constantin Stanislavski (1863–1938). Stanislavski's entire life was devoted to the theatre. He was an actor, writer, teacher, director, and most importantly, the developer of the Stanislavski System.

Constantin Sergeyevich Alexeiv (the "Stanislavski" is a pseudonym) was the son of a wealthy Moscow factory owner. After working for some years in his father's factory he developed an interest in acting. Stanislavski was taken as a child to plays, to the ballet and opera, and to the circus. He remembered the magic of the gas lights and the wonder of the performances. He made his debut on the stage on September 5, 1877, age 14, at a performance of four one-acts in celebration of his mother's birthday. From that time on he was possessed by the theatre. He began to direct as well as act and even at this early age he was interested in the rehearsal process of bringing a play to production.

By 1887 Stanislavski had decided to devote his life to the theatre. That same year he was involved in a production of *The Mikado.* Four months of rehearsal culminated in a dazzling production. "Stanislavski himself was aware of the value of the production to the group, in the agility and ease of body movement which resulted from the juggling, acrobatic and dancing required."[1] Throughout his career Stanislavski studied the movement of the actor and what he called the "rhythm" and "tempo" of a performance. These aspects as well as others which related to the process of acting, were to become his life's work—his method of acting.

The Stanislavski System, or "Method" as it was called by Lee Strasberg and his followers in the United States, was, and is today, the most revolutionary theory on acting and actor training to date. Perhaps because of his innate genius, or because of the time in history in which he worked, Stanislavski, like no other, was able to incorporate and synthesize many of the artistic theories on acting from Aristotle to Diderot. Then, with the aid of much scientific and psychological knowledge derived from Darwin, Freud, Pavlov, and others, he pushed further and deeper into our twentieth century understanding of the aesthetic experience called acting.

Stanislavski's System on acting was developed over a period of many years. He began first by criticizing his own acting and examples of the acting he witnessed by his contemporaries. He also found that in rehearsal he could devise certain exercises and techniques encouraging the cast to work as an ensemble and to "feel" their roles.

Much of the System developed from Stanislavski's attempts to understand rhythm—the inner or heart-felt rhythm of a character versus the external or physical rhythm in which most people move, react, and gesture. While investigating his role of General Imshin in *The Usurper of the Law,* Stanislavski made an important discovery.

> Here, once more, he approached the character from the outside. From his observations of an old man he discovered that space appears between the gums when the false teeth are removed. By moving his lower jaw forward he was able to give this effect. Then by trying to overcome the resultant lisp, he was obliged to speak more slowly than was his custom. The slow rhythm which was occasioned by the effort brought to his mind a very old man, and he was able to divine the inner emotion of the role.[2]

Stanislavski had discovered the physical and psychical connection. He described this method as "from the outer to the inner" and began to investigate and experiment further with the technical method of feeling in a physical sense in order to feel emotionally. Stanislavski realized that an actor could not learn to act by copying other actors. The actor must devise his own system for portraying the role. One thing of which he was sure was the connection between the physical and the emotional.

By 1897 Stanislavski was teamed with Vladimir Nemirovich-Danchenko to direct the newly formed Moscow Art Theatre. How fortunate it was that these two worked together, for their views on acting were the same. Danchenko declared:

> Any setting, gesture, or movement by an actor must depend directly on his internal, subjective life on the stage. The actor's crossing on the stage from right to left and vice versa must flow from the conduct of the character correctly conceived.[3]

In 1911 the Stanislavski System was officially adopted for use by the Moscow Art Theatre. Stanislavski was criticized for not describing his System in simple terms, a criticism which exists today and is the cause for much misinterpretation.

Volumes have been written on Stanislavski's life, his work, his philosophy, and his System. He has been the subject of praise, criticism, and controversy. Even today in the 1990s we interpret and reinterpret his notes trying to discover if his System does or does not work. Whether we laud or condemn Stanislavski's theories on stage performance, what we must accept is that at the center of the discussion of this man and his work there exists a wealth of information on the subject of actors and actor training. To dismiss this information is to turn our backs on what is certainly the most influential force in the theatre world of the twentieth century.

> The Stanislavski System is a means of manipulating levels of consciousness to achieve certain specific effects on the body, especially the illusion of spontaneity. It promises to give the actor expressive control over a living organism, his own body, in its mercurial diversity and surprising obstinacies. Among the techniques that Stanislavski proposes toward this end are the relaxation of the muscles, concentration of attention, public solitude, adaption, units and objectives, emotion memory, tempo-rhythm, the score of the role, and, definitively, the method of physical actions. Stanislavski's theories defy tidy summary because they

take into account the complexity of higher organisms, including the phenomenon of double or multiple consciousness. As he clarified the implications of contemporary psychophysiological theory in his own mind, Stanislavski adjusted his emphases to suit the emerging facts of life. His System, therefore, cannot be comprehended without his science.[4]

For Stanislavski, the method of physical actions was the culmination of his life work in the theatre, and for those interested in stage movement, it represents a strong foundation on which all modern theories of stage movement rest.

Briefly, the method of physical actions grew out of Stanislavski's interest and belief in the idea that certain stimuli could cause an outward or physical action based on an internal memory or feeling. Stanislavski experimented with levels of consciousness through concentration and relaxation techniques. He was attempting to control the subconscious, a task he knew was virtually impossible, yet not altogether so. He knew that physical actions could affect the subconscious to the point of "inner truth." "Why not," he contemplated, "reproduce those same actions for the desired result time after time?" This was his greatest discovery and, having come late in his career, it represented what Sonia Moore calls "the heart of his System."[5]

In *Creating a Role,* Stanislavski explains the chain of events through which the method of physical actions comprises a score of the role.

> With time and frequent repetition, in rehearsal and performance, this score becomes habitual. An actor becomes so accustomed to all his objectives and their sequence that he cannot conceive of approaching his role otherwise than along the lines of the steps fixed in the score. Habit plays a great part in creativeness: it establishes in a firm way the accomplishments of creativeness.... Habit creates second nature, which is a second reality. The score automatically stirs the actor to physical action.[6]

The method of physical actions is based on improvisations developed and executed by the actor and based on his psychological objectives and the given circumstances of events of the scene. As the actor repeats each event while in the state of psychological truth of the character, he begins to construct a chain of actions. The actor's body through kinesthetic memory is forming a learned awareness of movement patterns and detailed business. The inner workings of the actor (the psychological, emotional, and intellectual aspects of the character) are strengthened by the physical actions. The score of which Stanislavski spoke is like a musical score in that it represented a direction or a scenario. The actor must work to find the proper tone of speaking and moving as well as the appropriate textural quality, atmosphere, and rhythm-tempo. The method of physical actions provides a skeleton on which the actor can create his role.

In the United States, the System became known as the "Method," and it changed the style of American acting. Through the teachings of Stanislavski himself, and such protégés as Richard Boleslavsky, Lee Strasberg, Harold Clurman, Stella Adler, Sonia Moore and others, it is safe to say that he has been the most influential figure in acting in the twentieth century.

Many who studied under Stanislavski and those who studied his System have had quite different interpretations of his theory. Violent disagreements have taken place over his meaning of "feelings," "naturalism," and "physical actions." One such disagreement resulted in the break-up of Lee Strasberg and Stella Adler. Controversy still surrounds the interpretations of Stanislavski's System.

The phrase "method actor" has, since the 1960s, taken on a less than positive connotation. Synonymous with mumbling speech, introspection to the point of psychoanalysis, and movements which have meaning only to the inner mind of the actor, the "method" has, in effect, been on trial. This is unfortunate since it appears that Stanislavski is the natural and direct descendant of a long line of acting theorists who struggled for truth, beauty, and art in the theatre. Hopeful signs appear, however, and new interpretations of the System are being introduced to young students of acting. They, like those who take a second look at Stanislavski's System, find a master of the technique of acting.

Since Stanislavski's death a new group of theorists have emerged to practice their ideas on eager actors. It is ironic that, unlike our ancient ancestors who placed little emphasis on the training of the body, the new theorists seem obsessed with the body, its expressiveness, its

flexibility, and its organic makeup. F.M. Alexander, Moshe Feldenkrais, Antonin Artaud, Rudolf Laban, Ida Rolf, Alexander Lowen—
each hailed the body as the prime means of expression. But according
to the new theorists, the body must be retrained and restructured in
order for it to reach levels of truth in art.

> Our current views on acting seem to reverse the anxiety that seventeenth
> century rhetoricians expressed with regard to the flow of the passions: in-
> stead of worrying about how to cap the gusher, as they did, modern
> actors wonder where to drill. Contemporary psychology has utterly
> transformed our image of the body. We believe that spontaneous feel-
> ings, if they can be located and identified, must be extracted with
> difficulty from beneath the layers of inhibition that time and habit have
> deposited over our natural selves, selves that lie repressed under the
> rigidifying sediment of stress, trauma, and shame. We tend, therefore,
> to see our bodies as damaged by the kinds of lives we have lived.[7]

Stanislavski fully understood the problems that confronted the actor. He was able to define questions, concerns, and techniques for the
actor's needs in a way that had not been done before. He had an astute
eye for the details of life and an understanding of how to highlight those
details on the stage. At the time of his death he was still working on his
System. The System, like an actor's experience, continued to grow and
to evolve. Through his techniques and exercises such as emotion
memory, magic if, concentration of attention, public solitude, sensory
recall, and the method of physical actions, modern actors have been
freed of stereotyped and antiquated methods of acting and acting styles.
Stanislavski was able to encourage the actor into the twentieth century,
a time which, by its diversity, demanded a new approach to acting and
stage movement.

Stanislavski may well be the most influential acting theorist of the
twentieth century, yet he is not without his rivals. One such rival was
contemporary and fellow actor and director Vsevolod Meyerhold.

8. Meyerhold's Biomechanics

In his chronicle of Meyerhold's work James Symons states, "It may be argued that Vsevolod Emilevich Meyerhold stands in relation to the modern theatre as do his contemporaries Isadora Duncan, Igor Stravinsky, and Walter Gropius to dance, music, and architecture."[1] Vsevolod Meyerhold was at the cutting edge of changes in theatre with special contributions in the areas of acting, stage movement, and directing. It is unfortunate that he was not able to live to see the full fruition of his bold and exciting ideas. Until recently much of his work has been clouded in mystery and misinterpretation and he was overshadowed by the works of Stanislavski. Meyerhold's life, his political affiliation, and the revolutionary climate in Russia during the first three decades of this century appear interwoven, each influencing the other.

On January 28 (old style)[2], 1874, in the small village of Pensa southeast of Moscow, Vsevolod Emilevich Meyerhold's life began.[3] Born of bourgeois native German parents he was christened Karl Theodore Kasimir. His mother assured that he had a proper education and encouraged him to study piano. Another part of his education included a study of the theatre. Meyerhold's small hometown was often a stop for touring actors, many of whom were quite reputable and famous. Though Pensa was not an important town, it did lie along major trade routes. The busy atmosphere of the town, along with the fact that the actors were often entertained at his home, most surely influenced his later interests in the excitement of the theatre.

Meyerhold's growing fascination with the theatre was matched by his interest in politics and the socialist critics. By the age of twenty-one he was off to Moscow to study law at the University, but this career was short lived. The ballet, the opera, and the theatre won his attention and he left the study of the law for a study of the theatre at the Moscow Philharmonic Society. It was at the Philharmonic that Meyerhold first encountered his teacher, Vladimir Nemirovich-Danchenko. Danchenko said that Meyerhold's acting was "exceptional" and that he was capable of a wide variety of powerful characterizations.[4]

In 1899 upon graduation Meyerhold was awarded the silver medal for acting, an honor he shared with Olga Knipper, Anton Chekhov's future wife. During that same year Meyerhold was invited to join the newly formed Moscow Popular Art Theatre under the direction of Danchenko and Constantin Stanislavski. "Thus, at the age of twenty four . . . Meyerhold began his professional career as a charter member of a company that was to become world famous and the very antithesis of all that Meyerhold himself would eventually represent."[5] That company, of course, was later named the Moscow Art Theatre.

Although Meyerhold was active at the MAT, both as an actor and, at times, as assistant director, it became increasingly clear that his style of theatre was incompatible with the style of realism practiced by Stanislavski and Danchenko. In 1902 Meyerhold left the MAT under unexplained circumstances. The major differences were aesthetic, but an important financial matter may have been the cause as well.

Though Meyerhold publicly denied in the *Moscow Courier* that his reasons for leaving had anything to do with contracts or wages, it does seem that this may have forced his resignation. However, he was not long absent from the theatre. Later that fall, he organized his own company, the Comrades of the New Drama, and began directing. Meyerhold experimented in the Symbolist movement of theatre hoping to discover a new realm of stylized theatre. Stanislavski continued to be interested in Meyerhold's work and intently followed his career.

> The difference between us lay in the fact that I only strained toward the new, without knowing any of the ways for reaching or realizing it, while Meierhold [i.e., Meyerhold] thought that he had already found new ways and methods which he could not realize partly because of material

conditions and partly due to the weak personnel of his troupe.... I decided to help Meierhold in his new labors, which as it seemed to me then, agreed with many of my dreams at the time.[6]

Once again Stanislavski and Meyerhold attempted to work together at the Moscow Art Theatre Studio, but aesthetic differences prevailed. The union was useless. Meyerhold upheld the importance of the director, while Stanislavski felt that the creativity of the actor was being overshadowed by the director. For Meyerhold the actor merely served a purpose for the director. On the other hand, Stanislavski maintained that the director's sole duty was to open the way for the actor. Ironically, the two men did not work together again until some thirty-three years later on what was to become the final production for both.

Much of the avant-garde work being performed in Russia was referred to as Symbolist or Impressionist Theatre, a style which did not describe Meyerhold's work. He quickly drew attention as the "enfant terrible" of the Russian theatre. Despite the controversy which surrounded his works, he was successful and continued to gain recognition as an innovator and creative genius.

In 1907 Meyerhold was approached by V.A. Teliakovsky, the director of the Imperial Theaters, a chain of playhouses which dominated commercial theatrical enterprises in Russia. Teliakovsky wanted someone who could bring new energy to the theatre and Meyerhold was the choice. Meyerhold accepted and began as director. During his years at the Imperial Theaters, 1908 to 1917, Meyerhold altered many of his radical ideas on staging and theatre practice. He became less controversial and eccentric, and he struggled with the persistent question: Whose province is the theatre, the actor or the director?

During this period Meyerhold published articles on the theatre, one of which was "The Theatre: Its History and Technique." In it he outlined his break with realism and naturalism. He foresaw a new theatre in which the audience and the actor together developed a "willing suspension of disbelief." This momentary suspension of disbelief was not aimed at realism, but at symbolism. Meyerhold believed that the actor performed through his own body—a concept which later developed into his Biomechanics theory and the training workshop for the "cabotin" or actor. All of this promising work was cut short on

February 27, 1917. The Russian Revolution began and, for Meyerhold, as well as for the world, nothing would be the same again.

It is important to note that at the time of the Revolution almost 80 percent of the population of Russia was illiterate. The theatre, like public readings and church rites, played a large part in shaping the public consciousness. The theatre was a source not only of diversion and entertainment but of enormous social impact. After the Revolution the theatre became almost wholly political, serving as a platform for productions which proclaimed the rights of the proletariat. For this reason the theatre of Russia during the 1920s was exciting, fervently struggling to find its voice. Stanislavski and Danchenko supported the conventional Russian theatre, the one apart from politics. Meyerhold followed the Futurists, and wished to remake the theatre. The work was generally accepted at first as avant-garde, but by 1932 it was associated with aesthetic movements in the West and fell under discredit.

> After the Revolution Meyerhold came to the forefront with startling staging which dispensed with the curtain, extended the stage into the illuminated auditorium, and employed bare constructivist settings. He was extremely eclectic in his methods, borrowing heavily from primitive and oriental practice. Frequently he rewrote or reorganized classic plays to fit the mood of his own theatrical motif.[7]

Over the years of his career Meyerhold underwent many philosophical changes. Beginning with an admiration of the theatre of Appia, Wagner, and Maeterlinck, he soon moved to accept the Futurists' machine aesthetic. While employed by the Imperial Theaters he catered to the intellectual elite but never accepted their politics. His involvement in political theatre reached its peak when in 1918 he joined the Communist Party, a decision he never repudiated despite the strife he faced over the years.

Meyerhold was passionately in love with the theatre, an emotion which was stronger than his party politics. The Russia of the 1930s under Stalin was an environment which allowed no room for one who doubted the party-dictated ideology, and Meyerhold was beginning to be restless with the dictates of the times. He continued to work, to innovate, and to develop new styles of acting and staging. At times he pushed the bounds of acceptability and so became increasingly controversial.

Meyerhold was arrested in June 1939, after delivering a speech denouncing Socialist Realism. Only two weeks after his arrest his wife's mutilated body was found in their apartment. After Meyerhold's arrest he was listed as "missing" and he was never heard from again. Some speculated that he was alive and in Siberia. Still other reports stated that he died in 1942, but in 1961 it was officially announced that he had died on February 2, 1940, in Moscow. No cause of death was given and it was assumed that his end came violently.

Meyerhold's life is an example of commitment to an art and to an ideology. He represented the avant-garde, and like so many other theorists, he was misquoted, misread, and misinterpreted. He sought a public laboratory in which his experiments in alternative acting styles could be realized. Perhaps his most significant contribution to the theatre which followed him was in the area of what came to be called Meyerhold's Theory of Biomechanics.

> Biomechanics was a system of actor training that Meyerhold devised shortly after the Revolution. Although not always clearly understood, it received wide attention during the 1920s and 1930s due to Meyerhold's unique position as the foremost, revolutionary, avant-garde director. Curiously, Meyerhold's own conceptions about Biomechanics, which were almost unchanged throughout his career, appeared to be both grandiose and seemingly modest. While maintaining that the mastery of Biomechanics afforded the actor all the essential skills necessary for scenic movement — skills that would take the ordinary actor nearly a lifetime to learn, he relegated his own class in Biomechanics at the Meyerhold Workshop to a status equal to modern dance, or *eurhythmics*. Partly because of this apparently paradoxical attitude and partly due to the similar theoretical foundations of Meyerhold's training program and his early post-revolutionary system of acting, Soviet and Western critics were frequently confused as to Biomechanics theatrical function and application.[8]

Meyerhold's concept of actor training or Biomechanics began in the pre–Revolutionary years of his own training in Russia. Although Meyerhold had great respect for Stanislavski, he opposed his concept of theatre and the naturalistic movement of which Stanislavski was a leading proponent. Although naturalism and Russian realism were the dominant conventions of the theatre, the symbolists were active through the works of Meyerhold, Alexander Blok, Emile Verhaeren, and Maurice Maeterlinck. After the Revolution the way was made clear for innovation and Meyerhold took his chance to rebel against the constraints of the day and to experiment with his own style of theatre. Meyerhold commented on the acting of the Naturalistic theatre:

> The naturalistic theatre teaches the actor to express himself in a finished, clearly defined manner; there is no room for the play of allusion or for conscious understatement. That is why one so often sees overacting in the naturalistic theatre; it knows nothing of the power of suggestion.[9]

Acting, stage movement, indeed the art of the theatre as a whole, should do more, Meyerhold believed, than represent life in a realistic manner. He sought to stylize and conventionalize the theatre. Changes in the theatre were not limited to the works of Meyerhold in Russia. In fact a variety of "isms" sprang up during the period of 1915 to 1930 across Europe. Those "isms" included Cubism, Surrealism, Symbolism, Dadaism, Futurism, and especially, Constructivism. Constructivism was the movement which most clearly related to the Biomechanical works of Meyerhold in post–Revolutionary Russia. Most of the terms were first applied to new trends in the visual arts. Similar titles were given to innovations in literature. Many such titles had a carry-over effect in describing the changes which were occurring rapidly in the theatre arts.

Meyerhold was most active in his application of Biomechanics and Constructivism between 1922 and 1925. Meyerhold's Constructivism related to the arrangement of "nonrepresentational platforms, ramps, turning wheels, trapezes, and other objects to create a 'machine for acting,' more practicable than decorative."[10] The post–Revolutionary period was a machine age in Europe and the United States as well. There was a great interest in the utility and function of the machine, which allowed for everything from industry to the human labor force to become more efficient and productive. To achieve this productivity, this essence, Meyerhold looked to the Greeks first. The Greeks, he felt, were the most effective in the stylization of theatre. Next he studied the theatre styles of Japan, India, and China. He was especially interested in the writings of Gordon Craig and the idea of puppet theatre.

> From all of these varied sources Meyerhold drew ideas which helped to mould his own conception of theatre as mime, movement, and rhythm

in opposition to the prevailing cult of literature and 'authentic emotions.' Greatest and most persistent was Meyerhold's debt to the Italian *commedia dell'arte*.[11]

Meyerhold's work with *commedia dell'arte* came at the Meyerhold Studio in St. Petersburg as a result of his longtime interest in the style of acting. In fact, it was because of his interest in commedia that he came to the conclusion that:

> Movement is the most powerful means of theatrical expression. The role of movement is more important than any other theatrical element. Deprived of dialogue, costume, footlights, wings and auditorium and left only with the actor and his mastery of movement, the theatre remains the theatre. The spectator understands the theatre's intent through the actor's movements.[12]

From this interest in the power of movement Vladimir N. Soloviev, who was experienced with commedia styles as well as the Spanish theatre of the seventeenth century, assisted Meyerhold in developing three courses to be taught at his workshop. Soloviev conducted a course on commedia, and a series of interludes or Sixteen Etudes, as they were called, were used as practice material. Meyerhold taught the course called "Movement on Stage" which was the foundation work for the Biomechanics system. Each etude or exercise was to teach students the principles of stage movement in various stage blocking patterns and body positions. These etudes were outlined as:

1. How an actor should move in a circle, square, or triangle.

2. How the alternation of the numbers of even or odd characters affects the style of acting.

3. How the relationship of actor and acting space can be affected by movement.

4. How the time/space realities of the stage can be contrasted with those of life.

5. How pauses in movement can be made more effective.

6. How to work with stage properties; and

7. How the use of small versus large gestures can affect the spectator.[13]

According to Meyerhold these etudes should prepare the actor for all expressive situations which he or she might experience on the stage.

It is interesting to note that there seemed to exist during this time a belief that the uses of the machine were virtually limitless. This idea pervaded the work of many theorists such as Meyerhold. He sought to reduce the aesthetics and practice of acting to a systematized routine which, when perfected, would grant the actor limitless virtuosity. Meyerhold hoped that the theatre of Russia (which he characterized as a political and social tool) would go through the same type of changes that were being experienced in Soviet society. The collectivization and industrialization of Soviet society brought a sincere hope and belief in a better life. This hope may have been somewhat naive and innocent at first, yet it encouraged a generation onward. The Soviet culture was going through rapid and massive changes during the post–Revolutionary years. No one, it seems, took time to question the benefits of those changes.

Another prominent influence on Meyerhold's early Biomechanical work was the American inventor Frederick W. Taylor (1856–1915). Taylor was responsible for the study of scientific management during the early 1900s and the results of his work became widely accepted in Europe by 1910. Lenin himself was an advocate of Taylorism, as it was called.

Taylor's research findings represented the essence of a preoccupation with the efficiency of the machine age. He found, after studying each work unit of a production line, that the human worker's physical movements were the least efficient and productive of the entire factory. He further reported that the human worker wasted valuable time and energy on "superfluous and awkward motions, causing a premature strain in his muscles and generally lowering his work output."[14]

Taking into account the rhythm of the work performed, the type of physical movements required to perform the task, and other elements such as fatigue and rest/recovery, Taylor developed the study of motion economy. His work was reduced to seven fundamentals of human body principles after his death in 1915. Those seven principles are:

1. Smooth, continuous, curved movements of the hands.

2. Hands working simultaneously to complete their actions.

3. Both hands should never be idle at the same time.

4. Arm motions should be made in opposite, symmetrical directions, and simultaneously.

5. All motions should be confined to those which require the least amount of muscle exertion.

6. Muscles should contract using positive muscle groups as opposed to antagonistic muscle groups.

7. Rhythmic movements are generally preferred.[15]

Meyerhold was intrigued by these principles of Taylor's motion economy and further studied these results through the works of the Soviet Taylorist A.K. Gastev (1881–1941). Meyerhold, no doubt, was searching for an economical system through which actors' movements could be analyzed, trained, practiced, and performed.

If the period from 1900 to 1930 was a machine age, it was also an age of scientific innovation and revolution. The fields of psychology and medicine, as well as biology, physiology, chemistry, and physics, witnessed great changes, and much was added to the body of existing knowledge. Much of the work in psychology during those early years rested in the works of those conducting research in reflexology, or objective psychology. These psychologists rejected the findings which stated that behavior was explained through the unconscious. Such noted psychologists during the time were American psychologist William James (1842–1910), who examined the nature of emotion; Russian Vladimir Bekhterev (1857–1927), who worked towards a discovery of laws which governed reflexology and behavior; and Russian physiologist and psychologist Ivan Petrovich Pavlov (1849–1936), who won the Nobel Prize for studies in reflex excitation and inhibition.

> Underlying this new science resided the ideological assumption that external conditions determine human nature and that objectively controlled manipulation of the physical environment will alter the inward man. This science denies, in short, that a meaningful distinction can be drawn between the psychological and the physical or, for that matter, between the vital and the mechanical.[16]

Although it is unclear whether Meyerhold was a student of those objectivists, it is certain that the theories were widely circulated among scientists and in related fields throughout the Soviet Union after the Revolution. The significance of the results of reflexology for the theatre theoreticians can be seen in the following statement.

> All manifestations of brain function can be reduced to muscular movement. Emotions are merely intensified reflexes. Thoughts are merely

reflexes. Reflex action thus constitutes the basis of all behavior, spontaneous and acquired, muscular and mental. In fact, the convenient
terms mental and physical simply describe two aspects of an indivisible
phenomenon — life.[17]

In short, psychology can be reduced to physiology. For Meyerhold this
was proof that the actor need not delve into the introspective,
psychological, emotional part of the character. Find the physical or
physiological first, and the emotional will follow naturally.

The final major influence on Meyerhold's theory of Biomechanics
was Constructivism, which served more as a backdrop for Biomechanics
than as innovation. Constructivism was a style of theatre, just as it was
a style of painting or sculpture in the visual arts. In the Soviet theatre
Constructivism was at its peak between 1922 and 1926 and embraced
ideas on staging, directing, scene design, and acting.

> In Meyerhold's mechanistic vision of the theatre as factory and
> schoolroom — the use of the fastest and most efficient methods
> (Taylorism) to produce a predetermined audience reaction (reflexology),
> we find a total emphasis on work output — the manufacture of effects in
> the spectator, creating a desired state of mind. Allowing for the fact that
> there was a finite number of effects and states of mind, the Construc-
> tivist director/engineer was free to calibrate the theatrical components
> at his disposal (dramatic text, staging areas, scenery, properties, costum-
> ing, lighting, styles of acting, speech, music, tempo, etc.) in nearly inex-
> haustible combinations, toward a single goal. In this, the constructivist
> director worked much like Taylor, who approached each task differently,
> seeking a unique strategy for the execution of economic and efficient
> movements.[18]

Meyerhold chose to educate his Biomechanically trained actors
through the style of theatre backdrop characteristic of Constructivism.
He approached his directing much like an engineer approaches his
work. Seeking harmony, unity, and economy, Meyerhold synthesized
the principles of reflexology and Taylorism, then adapted them to the
needs of the actor, both in training and in performing. Meyerhold's
theatre of the Constructivist period employed purely theatrical sources
such as: circus, gymnastics, Oriental theatre, puppets and marionettes.
Staging was simplified and often a variety of levels were used to offer
the actor an interesting space to move within and about.

In 1922, in his workshop seminars, Meyerhold schooled his actors-in-training in Biomechanics, fencing, boxing, acrobatics, classical ballet, modern dance, juggling, voice/diction, and Dalcroze eurhythmics. Biomechanics was to be the educational link which connected all aspects of training for the actor. Biomechanics was to provide for the actor to be a worker in an acting machine. "Perhaps the basic principle of biomechanics . . . was the conscious dualism between the actor's idea of the role and his performance of it."[19]

An actor trained in Biomechanics was distinguished by his athletic, energetic, and pantomimic training. Actor training was presented in a new form, one which had a base in science and industry. Meyerhold concluded that Diderot's writings were in agreement with Biomechanics in that "the expert who has mastered a 'mechanical craft' will grasp the whole nature of a process, no motion of the hand will escape him, for he will easily distinguish a meaningless flourish from an essential precaution."[20]

Although Meyerhold held his theories on Biomechanics as less important than other aspects of his theatre practice, it is what he is best remembered for today. Like many theoreticians, his ideas were interpreted, reinterpreted, misinterpreted, and often misunderstood. Meyerhold sought to bring a theatre of simplicity to the people, a kind of theatre of the people and for the people. Perhaps Meyerhold's greatest legacy has been the kind of Biomechanical and Constructivist approach which is evident in many avant-garde and Theatre of the Absurd productions of the post–World War II era.

> Like the victims of Meyerhold's tragic farces, Absurdist characters appear as mere marionettes, helpless puppets without a will of their own, passively at the mercy of blind fate and meaningless circumstances. The spectators in the Theatre of the Absurd are thus confronted with a grotesquely heightened picture of their own world.[21]

Biomechanics was a means to an end. It was designed as a clear, scientific and methodological system through which the actor could train his responses, physical and mental, to meet the needs of any role in any play he was chosen to portray. The goal of Biomechanics was to train and condition the reflex actions of the actor to their peak effectiveness ultimately granting the actor the appearance of realism or second nature.

Meyerhold interpreted the actor's task of characterization as occurring from the outside in. The actor, as Meyerhold taught in his workshop, was involved in a process of reverse reality. That is, to experience fear, for example, the actor must first run, then express fear. In life the reverse, of course, would be true. The actual involvement in the action could cause the reaction, and this could be accomplished through physical or movement means. Meyerhold explained that his Biomechanical exercises followed a cycle which began with (1) the intention, or the preparation for an action, (2) the realization, or the action itself, and (3) the subsequent intention, which was a new preparation for that action which followed.

Biomechanics became the means through which Meyerhold could redirect the creative process. Edward Braun, author of *Meyerhold on Theatre,* states Meyerhold's vision: "The art of the actor consists in organizing his material; that is, in his capacity to utilize correctly his body's means of expression."[22] Biomechanics was for Meyerhold "the essential basis of every actor's training."[23]

John Martin, noted dance critic, outlined the Meyerhold "method" of actor training in a November 1930, issue of *Theatre Guild Magazine* just as the Meyerhold company was about to make its first American tour.

> Biomechanical actors men and women alike, are taught, first of all, to box; for Meyerhold sees the problems of a play as closely akin to those of a boxing match with its firmness of stance, its alertness, its exchange of blows, the continuous physical give and take, clean cut and accurately timed. Many traces of this type of training are to be found in the carriage of the actors, particularly in the classes devoted to exercises in biomechanics as such.[24]

Martin goes on to comment on the apparent relaxation of the actors as they rehearse and go through their exercises. This, he explains, is due to the fact that they are not burdened by the psychological weight of their character study.[25] During the visit of the company to the United States it was also noted that the exercises were performed to music to aid in the establishment of proper tempo for the moment. The strenuousness of the exercises was to develop strength, agility, and flexibility. The pantomime and dance work was to encourage the actor to move expressively, with proper phrasing, with a sense of beauty, grace, and flow, and to make all parts of the body sensitive to outside stimuli.

> The actor trained under this system does not learn to feel the life about him, but to see and touch it; he does not go about as his predecessors did seeking emotional experiences to store away against a future need, he bends all his labors to keeping his body alert and agile and his nervous responses keen.[26]

Meyerhold's method of actor training offered a viable alternative to the deeply introspective exercises proclaimed by Stanislavski. Meyerhold was close to Delsarte in his belief that the outward sign, not the inward urge, was the focus of acting. Yet, in common with Stanislavski, he felt the importance of interplay or relationships on stage. They also held similar attitudes on the importance of "the first time" experience in acting, though the channel through which this was achieved was quite different.

Perhaps Meyerhold was still at work on his Biomechanics at the time of his untimely and suspicious death. Perhaps, like Stanislavski, he was preparing to update his writings, thus clarifying and more clearly defining his theories for present and future readers. As John Martin stated in 1930,

> Biomechanics . . . is merely a tool in his hands, when his inventive mind has devised a better or a more useful one it will no doubt be superseded. With Meyerhold the Theatre is the thing: let the theories fall where they will.[27]

Meyerholds's influence can be seen in the avant-garde of today and in the training techniques of contemporary actors. He did much to change the scope of modern staging, acting, and audience participation. He believed in the expressive powers of movement and he schooled his actors in those devices. "If the avant-garde were given to looking backward, instead of by definition forward, it would surely recognize one of the fathers of modern theatre in Vsevolod Meyerhold."[28]

9. Postmodern Trends: Jerzy Grotowski

Theatre is the mirror image of the life and age of those theatre artists who live and work within a particular time and who are reacting against or in support of current trends. This is especially true of Jerzy Grotowski, a man who "seemed so much a summary of all that the avant-garde [of the 1960s] had absorbed from Zen, from happenings and from the work of Artaud."[1]

It has been more than twenty years now since the Western world was first exposed to the work of Jerzy Grotowski and his Polish Laboratory Theatre. According to Jennifer Kumiega in *The Theatre of Grotowski*, his work represented an almost "messianic" appearance in the West.[2] Because he is a contemporary it is difficult to evaluate the full range of his influence on the American theatre, or the theatre of Europe. But it is certain that he helped to shape the theatre of the 1960s and the 1970s with emphasis on acting, staging, and a theatrical invention which stripped it of all its "artistic kleptomania."[3]

Jerzy Grotowski was born in Rzeszow, Poland, a small town on the Eastern border, on August 11, 1933. He grew up with his mother (a schoolteacher) and his older brother. Early in World War II, at the age of six, he moved with his mother and brother to Nieadowski. Throughout the war Grotowski lived in the small, rural village and traveled daily back to Rzeszow to attend school, the same school at which his mother was a teacher.

Education played an important role in the early life of Grotowski, an education which was often interrupted by illness. In 1950 his family moved to Cracow where he completed his secondary education. At his mother's urging he applied for admission to the State Theatre School in Cracow as an acting major. His examination scores were only satisfactory, and so he had to compose an additional written paper for admission. The title of his paper was entitled "In What Way May Theatre Contribute to the Building of Socialism in Poland?" The paper was excellent and he was granted admission in October 1951.

In 1955 Grotowski completed his studies and earned his actor's diploma. That same year he published four articles on the art of the theatre. It was common practice with Poland's highly systemized education process to employ a graduate immediately after graduation. An exception was made in Grotowski's case, however, and he was allowed to attend a directing course at the State Institute of Theatre Art in Moscow. It was while he studied in Moscow that Grotowski came to admire and respect the works of Stanislavski, Vakhtangov, and Meyerhold. Stanislavski remained a powerful influence on Grotowski's work and approach to acting. Grotowski admits in *Towards a Poor Theatre* that "Stanislavski asked the key methodological questions."[4]

In 1956 Grotowski's ill health again interrupted his studies in Moscow and he was sent to Central Asia to recuperate. He became fascinated with Eastern philosophy and later, in 1970, he returned to Asia on a personal odyssey.

Grotowski returned to Poland late in 1956, and there he found great political changes. Poland was undergoing dramatic de–Stalinization and Grotowski, along with other artists and Party intellectuals, was swept into the liberal movement. The liberals were obsessed with independence from the Soviet Union, while the Party enthusiasts tried to placate the dominant Russians. Grotowski became more and more involved with the activist movement, later admitting that he had wanted to be a "political saint."[5]

Grotowski remained in Cracow during the period of his political activism. He began his professional directing career in 1959 in Opole, and his first important debut was Ionesco's *The Chairs*. This represented an openness for Western writers and production of Western plays in Poland. It was during these early years of his directing career that Grotowski experimented with Meyerhold's Constructivism as well as the use of masks and film montage as part of his productions.

It was during 1959 that Grotowski met Marcel Marceau in Paris. Marceau later proved a great influence on him. He also encountered Ludwik Flazen, theatre and literary critic, someone who would later become an influential colleague of Grotowski and the Polish Laboratory Theatre. In May of 1959 Flazen contacted Grotowski with the offer of the directorship of the Theatre of Thirteen Rows, a small avant-garde theatre in Opole.

> ...Grotowski put forward proposals for the following season's repertoire, and a tour of the major Polish cities. Most importantly, he laid down conditions for the establishment of the theatre, including a free hand in the selection of the repertoire and group, the establishment of the post of literary director, a permanent subsidy, and a budget level permitting work without continual upsets. These conditions which were accepted, together with the subsidy granted by the Opole People's Council, permitted the establishment of what was called "the only professional experimental theatre in Poland."[6]

Grotowski began the company with nine actors, two of whom were women, and with the emphasis on ensemble playing. The actors served in many off-stage roles, sometimes as stage manager or stagehand. Later, in 1961, Grotowski formed the Laboratory Theatre with three of the original members from the Theatre of Thirteen Rows. By 1964 his company was complete with Ludwik Flazen as literary director.

The Laboratory Theatre received only a small subsidy, thus forcing a financial hardship on the company. "Poverty was at first a practice of this theatre; only later was it raised to the dignity of aesthetics."[7] Grotowski saw a new style of theatre and this was, in part, due to the political and artistic climate in Poland in the post war years.

> The period from 1939 [to] 1956 had been one of almost total stagnation in the theatrical world in Poland. Not only were all theatres closed down during the war, and many theatre artists killed or imprisoned, but even after liberation there was an enforced programme of Socialist Realism.... This, combined with a policy of centralized administration, succeeded in destroying all the creative independence that makes theatre so valuable. But with the general relaxation of restrictions in the mid-fifties, the Polish theatre began to flourish again.[8]

In the late 1950s and early 1960s the influx of Western theatre styles was making its mark on Grotowski and the Polish theatre. This was particularly true of the Absurdist movement. Grotesque absurdism had long been established in Poland dating back to the works of Stanislav Witkiewicz. The idea of Western absurdism was not totally new to the Poles; in fact, it served to stimulate interest in the theatrical traditions of Poland. It was the new theatrical freedom which Poland, and Grotowski, sought from the West. Grotowski was, by the 1960s, interested in opposing mainstream ideas. This was evident in his theatrical statements and practice. Grotowski began to reevaluate the actor. Should acting follow the psychological and intuitive style of the Stanislavski system or should it follow the theory of intellectual theatre? Grotowski

> ...wanted the actor to be elevated from merely one of several factors in a theatrical event to the essence of theatre itself: simultaneously there should be a reduction of the artistic means of expression extraneous to the actor. This basic premise became known as "poor theatre."[9]

In 1962 Grotowski directed his most stylized work to date, *Akropolis.* This production led to a growing interest in Grotowski's style of poor theatre. Students came to Poland for apprenticeship and much was written in the West about the production. This led to Grotowski's work finally being accessible outside of Poland. Grotowski's next production was based on *Dr. Faustus* by Christopher Marlowe. His company was invited to perform in Belgium and Holland in 1964, and in Paris in 1965. However, political conditions in Poland did not allow Grotowski and the Lab Theatre to accept the invitations. Instead, Grotowski moved his company from Opole to Wroclaw, a new home which proved very beneficial.

Grotowski was allowed to travel throughout Europe giving demonstrations and attending festivals without his company. In August 1965 he traveled to London at the invitation of director Peter Brook. The next month he published his manifesto, "Towards a Poor Theatre," in the Polish magazine *Odra.* In 1966 the Laboratory Theatre began an international theatre tour which lasted until 1970. Their tour in Europe included Holland, Italy, Yugoslavia, France, and Great Britain, and in the West, Mexico, and the United States. Despite growing worldwide acceptance of Grotowski's work and support of his artistic theories, he still lacked acceptance in his own country. His views as expressed in his work and writings were regarded suspiciously.

In the years following the early 1970s Grotowski continued to explore, invent, investigate, and develop his "poor theatre" and his methods of actor training as well as actor performance. His company completed other international tours, including successful tours to the United States. Between the years 1978 and 1984 the Lab Theatre was in a state of continual change. Most significant among the changes were the pressures of political upheaval in Poland at that time. Although this was an active period for the Lab Theatre, it seemed to have lost much of its cohesive force. Instead, there was a variety of types of work and projects being offered under the sponsorship of the Lab Theatre.

Much of Grotowski's emphasis by the late 1970s was centered around his idea of "active culture," something which he considered to be the most significant work of the Lab to date. This concept of the "active culture" describes a first person experience with a creative act, like writing a book or performing in a play. This is opposed to "passive culture" in which one only observes. The elements of "active culture" as Grotowski describes them are "action, reaction, spontaneity, impulse, song, compatibility, music-making, rhythm, improvisation, sound, movement, truth and the dignity of the body."[10] This represents a one-to-one experience which goes beyond the actor-audience relationship. This is a shared experience which embodies the essence of creativity, and it is not necessarily related to performance.

In 1980 Grotowski left the group to pursue his own travels and individual studies. Political events in Poland during 1980 and 1981 led to increased tension and an atmosphere charged with hope for positive change in the country. But increased support for Solidarity led to a crackdown on freedoms, accessibility to the media, and rationing. Between 1981 and 1982 two key members of the Lab Theatre died after long illnesses. The loss of these two was deeply felt by Grotowski as well as other members of the Lab Theatre. Also, during December 1981, a curfew was declared and the theatres were closed. In 1982 Grotowski left Poland bound for Denmark. After a short stay in that country he departed for the United States where he remains today. In January of 1984 in the local Wroclaw newspaper the following appeared,

> The group of the Theatre of Thirteen rows, of the Institute of Actor's Research, of the Institute of the Actor, in other words the group of the

Laboratory Theatre, is determined on 31 August 1984, after exactly 25 years, to disband.[11]

If Grotowski had kept his company in Poland, the political climate of suspicious admiration surely would have curtailed and stunted its growth. Instead, through acceptance and interest from the West he has grown into one of the most influential forces in postwar theatre. The interest in Grotowski's theories and work of the Polish Laboratory Theatre continue to grow today. Grotowski once commented that Stanislavski did not live long enough to have his system called a true "method." At the time of his death Stanislavski was still evolving his system, still changing and speculating. Grotowski, it seems, continues to evolve, change, and speculate on the true nature of the theatre. His system cannot be called a true "method" either.

Grotowski has offered through the works of his Polish Laboratory Theatre a new concept of theatre and of the actor. In a broadcast for Polish secondary schools on Polish radio in 1979 he stated:

> The fact is that our activity — that of the Laboratory Theatre — is to do with a very altered concept of theatre, with the destruction of the boundaries of this concept. Our activity has in this respect become symbolic for many people.... Theatre may ... be a place where the division into those who only watch and those who only act can begin to disappear.[12]

Grotowski embodied many of the psychological and avant-garde trends of the 1960s. Many of his exercises employed mind-expanding exercises. Actors were submerged in strenuous senuous physical and emotional exercises. The result was to be a physical immediacy and a so-called "autoperformance" which blended the actor and character in such a way that both were intimately revealed.

> [A] continuing point of debate in modern theatre theory has been over whether the theatre should be viewed primarily as an engaged social phenomenon or as a politically indifferent aesthetic artifact; a significant amount of contemporary theoretical discourse can still be oriented in terms of this opposition. Until the mid–1960s, the theorists who inclined towards an autonomous view of the theatre frequently looked to Artaud as their central modern spokesman; then a major new influence appeared in the production and theories of the Polish director Jerzy

Grotowski, who by the end of the decade came to rival Stanislavski himself as a theorist of acting and a central figure of modern theatrical consciousness. Grotowski's international influence may be dated from the 1966 performance in Paris of *The Constant Prince,* at the invitation of Barrault, a dazzling production characterized by many French critics as the long-awaited fulfillment of "Artaudian Theatre."[13]

By many interpretations Grotowski represents the synthesis of most of the predominate theatre principles which have occurred since the Greeks. He sought archetypal images to replace the religious elements used by the ancients. He had great respect for the theatre of commedia dell'arte as well as that of Shakespeare. He was a student of the Stanislavski System, Meyerhold's Biomechanical essence, and the über-marionettes of Craig. He grew up with a profound belief in the political voice of theatre, yet he changed and reversed himself, striving for a theatre of freedom and exploration, one of autonomy. Theatre was for Grotowski always "performance rather than literature; action rather than language."[14]

Grotowski's early directing work established him as an explorer, a seeker, and someone who challenged accepted norms, always striving to find the most effective form for each particular production. The actor is the main focal point of a production. Therefore, Grotowski sought new ways of defining and challenging the age-old relationship of actor-character-spectator. Out of these early developments and experiments with the relationship he conceived of the idea of "poor theatre." This is reminiscent of what Meyerhold referred to in the early 1900s as "stripping the theatre" bare in order to arrive at its nucleus. Poor, according to Grotowski, refers to the bare essentials used in a theatrical production. Grotowski himself describes this style of theatre in the collection of essays, *Towards a Poor Theatre.*

> The elimination of stage-auditorium dichotomy is not the important thing—that simply creates a bare laboratory situation, an appropriate area for investigation.
> The essential concern is finding the proper spectator-actor relationship for each type of performance and embodying the decision in physical arrangements.
> We forsook lighting effects, and this revealed a wide range of possibilities for the actor's use of stationary light-sources by deliberate work with shadows, bright spots, etc. . . .

> We abandoned makeup, fake noses, pillow-stuffed bellies — every-
> thing that the actor puts on in the dressing room before
> performance. . . .
>
> Elimination of music (live or recorded) not produced by the actor
> enables the performance itself to become music through orchestration
> of voices and clashing objects. . . .
>
> The acceptance of poverty in theatre, stripped of all that is not
> essential to it, revealed to us not only the backbone of the medium, but
> also the deep riches which lie in the very nature of the art-form.[15]

The purity of Grotowski's theories was expressed clearly in the 1962
production of *Akropolis* which was performed along with *The Constant
Prince* and *Apocalypsis cum Figuris* on the American tour. The critical
review states that Grotowski uses "states of being" as opposed to the
more mundane "plot direction." Furthermore, it cites a focus on intensity above all in the production.[16] Finally,

> Grotowski has discovered that the smaller the audience the greater the
> intensity. The relationship between actor and audience is subtly altered
> from performer and spectator to a merging of personality in which each
> somehow acquires the identity of the other and suffers the same strife
> of soul.[17]

What was most philosophically evident in these productions was
the transcendence and purification of catharsis through opposition. This
implies that the essence of beauty is revealed through the grotesque.
The holy is made more spiritual through the blasphemous. For
Grotowski, this was revealed through the movements of the actor.
Movement represented a hierarchy in the actor's craft. It was the essence
of being, the essence of life, the essence of acting.

This insight came to Grotowski through his continual exploration
of the actor's craft, for Grotowski always stressed the actor. During his
developmental years Grotowski slowly stripped away all of the
nonessential elements of theatre. He struggled to abandon theatrical
barriers: spectator, stage, actor. This ultimately led to the autoperformance, "a mixture of autobiography and performance."[18] Grotowski
also refers to this as "translumination," a sort of trance through which
the actor reveals much of himself. This, Grotowski states, is "without
the least trace of egoism or self-enjoyment."[19]

Influenced by the Bohr Institute and using its methodology as a model, Grotowski sought to investigate the art of acting which he stated was neither a scientific discipline nor talent based solely on inspiration. He concluded that acting was made of a process of self-revelation, a process through which this self-revelation could be expressed (primarily through movement), and a process by which the actor rids himself of obstacles, both physical and psychic.

It is certain that Grotowski also was inspired by the works of Stanislavski, for he states that Stanislavski had the right questions. It is also certain that the works of Craig, Appia, and Meyerhold had a profound influence on Grotowski's theories concerning staging and movement. Artaud and the Theatre of the Absurd gave Grotowski the freedom to push his ideas to the limit. But perhaps an even more significant influence was the political and economic climate of Poland in the post–World War II era. Grotowski and his company worked in poverty. He was forced to strip down his productions to the bare essentials, and among these bare bones he found his greatest richness. Theatre could exist without costumes, sets, music, lighting; without all elements except the actor and the audience. The text itself was nonessential. Through improvisations, happenings, even "muttering," a dramatic event with profound intensity could be staged.

Much of the actor training in the Polish Laboratory Theatre focused on physical training. Movement constituted the essence of character. During the years 1959–1962 Grotowski introduced a series of training exercises which, he admits, have changed in their aims.

At first the exercises were "positive"—that is, those which added to, or objectively offered the actor a particular skill. Later Grotowski felt that these exercises were too result-oriented, only a means to an end. He changed the focus to what he referred to as "negative" exercises; those which eliminated the barriers between actor and performance. This latter focus aided the actor in overcoming inhibitions, fears, and resistance. The exercise series included eight points: (1) general warm-up, (2) exercises to loosen the muscles and the back, (3) exercises which focus on body changes (breathing, heartbeat, etc.), (4) movements which explore sensations of flight or weightlessness, (5) gymnastic-type exercises with leaps and somersaults, (6) extremity flexibility exercises, (7) mime exercises, and (8) studies in acting done while moving.

Another aspect of the physical training course included Dalcroze techniques to improve movements in opposition. Creative imagery exercises were also used such as: animal imagery, flower (birth, life, death), or walking barefoot over a variety of surfaces. For facial training Grotowski suggested the Delsarte exercise of "facial masks." All exercises were performed without interruption and without negative criticism from the group leader. The physical exercises were always accompanied later by a series of vocal exercises.

By 1966 the exercise program underwent definite changes. Grotowski began to incorporate animal imagery with physical exercises which were performed while the actor made some vocal intonation or sang. Action always preceded sound. Absolute concentration was demanded by all in the group. Some physical exercises were carried over from the 1959–1962 sessions such as the leaping, the back exercises, and the extremity exercises. Grotowski appeared to have added the slow motion and yoga techniques to many of the training tasks. The students worked while wearing very little clothing so as not to restrict any movements. They wore tennis shoes or worked barefooted. Grotowski assisted the students with the following advice, "Our whole body must adapt to every movement, however small. Everybody must proceed in his own way. No stereotype exercises can be imposed."[20]

In 1979 Daniel Cushman was invited to train with Grotowski's company in Poland. His description of the training method illustrates the similarities between the 1966 program and that which he attended.

> The instructions from the Lab asked each participant to bring as little as possible: a sleeping bag, eating utensils, and money for food.
> Everyone who didn't have tennis shoes was taken to buy some. They had planned for us to work barefoot but decided it was too cold.
> During the first few days the work space resembled an asylum or a production of *Marat/Sade* or *Akropolis* gone berserk. Much of the physical action seemed dangerously out of control.
> The intensity and relentlessness of the sound and movement in that confined place verged on being mesmeric.
> Most of the movement was deliberately angular, grotesque, intentionally asymmetrical like the physical vocabulary I had seen in Grotowski's productions.[21]

By the 1980s Grotowski's theories were generally accepted and he was considered by many to be the "new Stanislavski." A new vocabulary for actors emerged including "holy actor," "rich theatre," "catharsis," and, of course, "poor theatre."

The "Holy Theatre" was coined by Peter Brook in *The Empty Space*. To Brook, Holy Theatre is a "performance that aspires to the communication of intangibles..., universal levels of experience."[22] Grotowski defines the "holy" as a "secular holiness," one which is therapeutic and unmasks the true, internal, psychic, reality. The communication of intangibles was achieved through the movements and abstractions of movement of the character. The spontaneous and almost subconscious exploitation of movement was, for the "poor theatre" a guiding force. All exercises and theories concerning acting and performance stemmed from the point of catharsis and release of inner revelations through the physical expressions of the actor.

The Grotowski of the mid–1980s differed from the Grotowski of twenty years earlier. Grotowski's early work was similar to Brook's and Copeau's in that he was searching for a common universal language of the theatre. By reducing the theatre to its barest essentials he hoped to find "a language of sign and sounds."[23] Grotowski called these signals "ideograms" and stated that "New ideograms must constantly be sought and their composition appear immediate and spontaneous."[24]

Grotowski's "poor theatre" resembles Copeau's in their similar belief that the actor must sacrifice himself for the art. They differ, however, in that Copeau upheld that the actor must deny himself for the sake of unity through representation. Grotowski, on the other hand, asserted that the actor was revealed through the role. Grotowski maintained that the actor could, through release of his own psychic impulses, use his body as a psychologically expressive tool. This was therapeutic not only for the actor, but for the audience as well. Grotowski's ultimate goal was self-knowledge, whether the self was the actor or spectator. Copeau and Brook, on the other hand, sought a collective human truth.

During the 1970s Grotowski's attitude changed, vowing "no more performances." Instead he began to focus on paratheatrical, or purely experimental happenings. This represents, as Timothy Wiles states in *Theatre Event,* a shift away from the therapeutic, communal theatre.[25]

> The essential purpose of Grotowski's efforts remains the same: to encourage people to "disarm," to strip away the false veneer imposed on

them by socialization and reveal themselves as they truly are. The invitation to the audience which was formerly implicit in Grotowski's theatre is now explicit.[26]

No longer do the actors analyze themselves, thus asking the spectator to do the same. Now the actor creates a scenario through which the spectator can analyze himself directly. He has dropped much of the significant importance of the ideogram. He characterizes his theories as a "communion"; a ritual through which there can exist a kind of psychic healing. This is the essence of catharsis. In his recent "poor theatre" Grotowski has reached the level in which he encourages all to find their own levels of imagery through which they can deal with the cleansing of their lives.

> It is no longer a matter of the Christ-like self-sacrifice Grotowski saw in his "holy" actor, but of self-analysis leading to communal catharsis. . . . Grotowski's recent thought is based on disputable psychological and semilogical assumptions. The appeal of the concept of "holy theatre" in its various manifestations is neither logical nor scientific, but derives from its emphasis on catharsis, its belief that art (or something which approaches art, in the case of Grotowski's paratheatrical projects) can have a direct effect on its audience at the psychic level and that this effect, however it is defined, is ultimately of a health-giving nature.[27]

The philosophy of Grotowski's "poor theatre" is the "solemn act of collective exploration of the self."[28] In the poor theatre the actor is everything; he is the "living link," as Grotowski says, between the stage and the audience. In fact, there is often no distinction between performance space and spectator space. Theatre, for Grotowski, is a psychic experience, a ritualized experience. The theatre experience is both a sociological as well as a psychological process. He called upon actor and spectator to come together with souls bared, ready and open for self-analysis and self-realization. All this to provide a more humane world, a world with less tension and less pretense.

More specifically, Grotowski's "method,"[29] or process of actor training, is to encourage actors to open themselves to their own psychic truth. He never believed in prescriptions or methods to attain this, however. He firmly rejects any set of actions or exercises that are designed to lead to a specific result. In theatre there should be no photocopy. He rejects the idea that there exists a Stanislavski method or any other method. Training and performance in terms of Grotowski are more of an aesthetic, rather than a style or method of training.

To attempt to define or illustrate Grotowski's process of actor training, or work, is literally to define Grotowski's own, personal manner of working. His hope was that each actor would create his own, personal process.

> This means that although Grotowski believes that there exists a concrete path of research and training for the actor, the essential condition which qualifies this path or "method" is that it is individual and personal.[30]

Acting is not an acquisition of skills. The objectives of his system were to provide the actor with physical, vocal, and exploratory attitudes which would make him more open and revealing. The movement exercises were to grant the body more flexibility, sensitivity, strength, and agility. It was from the Oriental and East Indian theatre that Grotowski borrowed the idea of gesture and sign as language.

> Each gesture, each little motion is an ideogram which writes out the story and can be understood only if its conventional meaning is known. The spectator must learn the language, or rather the alphabet of the language, to understand what the actor is saying.[31]

The Oriental training process included (1) memorizing gestures, signs, and vocal signs, (2) body skills which reduced resistance to the work, and (3) acrobatic work which provided agility, spatial awareness, and defiance of gravity. This system was foremost in Grotowski's work until he realized that the "sacred" theatre could not exist in the West.

According to Grotowski Western society had long since lost touch with myth and with universal truth. As Robert Brustein commented in 1969, "American actors do not have the self-denial demanded by Grotowski's technique. To create this theatre, you must believe in something greater than theatre."[32]

Grotowski continued to believe that the highest aim of theatre was to change human perception and human relationships. The paratheatrical work included participants who were in need of a kind of theatrically fostered "psycho-drama."

This was work directed primarily towards the possibility of authentic spontaneity, and the release of a creative flow of energy: in other words it was a form of de-conditioning. But they were more proposing to involve directly members of the public.... At a deeper level they also needed to discover a structure which would permit the spectator-become-participant to reach quickly to a similar level of de-conditioning of their own.[33]

His concept of the "active culture" moved him further into a theatre Aristotle would describe as one in which the unities of time, place, and action exist. Grotowski's concept of theatre evolved into meaning an action which happened in a place or environment and was executed by a person, or actor. Why have scenery? Why have lights or props? The actual action being performed by the person in the original environment is more of a true theatrical event. Grotowski hoped for a blending of theatre and life, a time and place and an event which could bridge the gap between life and the reenactment of life.

The process of Grotowski's actor training cannot be easily outlined; it is a mood, an aesthetic, a religion, rather that an outline of steps that any actor-in-training can undergo. His philosophy is, however, one of truth, freedom, trust, and intensity. The objective of theatre is one of transformation — actor into participant/guide, and spectator into participant/follower. They enter into a sort of communion through which both reveal aspects of self and exit with more awareness and sensitivity to the life which surrounds them. All of this can be achieved through strict mental and physical sacrifice or vulnerability and through discipline.

Grotowski sought, in theory, what Stanislavski sought: attention to detail, true spontaneity, and emotional truth. He thought the theatre should and could be the "elevating" art of the twentieth century.

Theatre — through the actor's technique, his art in which the living organism strives for higher motives — provided an opportunity for what could be called integration, the discarding of masks, the revealing of the real substance: a totality of physical and mental reactions. This opportunity must be treated in a disciplined manner, with a full awareness of the responsibilities it involves.... This act, paradoxical and borderline, we call a total act. In our own opinion it epitomizes the actor's deepest calling.[34]

Three giants of the theatre of the twentieth century were Constantin Stanislavski, Vsevolod Meyerhold, and Jerzy Grotowski. Each was confronted in his own work yet each lived beyond his work in his unique contribution to the modern movement training of the actor.

Stanislavski's contributions lay in his System on acting and especially the method of physical actions. Meyerhold established himself in the area of movement training under the title of Biomechanics. Grotowski emerged as the avant-garde leader in movement training with his concept of the "holy actor" and his movement-actor training methods. In each of these three men there are many similarities.

Each organized his own company in an effort to establish a public laboratory, a place to experiment and promote his ideas.

Each had a strong background as an actor and a director.

Each valued movement as a basis and center for actor training and characterization.

Each worked to develop a new style of acting and staging.

Each felt that his technique could be used in any production of any play.

Each used a variety of physical work, such as flexibility exercises, gymnastic movements, relaxation techniques, mime, and psycho physical exercises in their movement training.

In the theatre of Stanislavski, Meyerhold, and Grotowski there are, however, some crucial differences. Stanislavski believed the director's task was to free the actor. Meyerhold stressed the director's role where Grotowski held that the actor was the performance. Meyerhold viewed acting (and stage movement) as a means to an end, and as a science. Grotowski, on the other hand, was interested in the honesty and catharsis of movement and acting. Acting, for Grotowski was not so much of a science, a thing to experience, to be studied and proven, but a psychological quest, a self-actualization. Stanislavski believed that movement was the beginning point of characterization. Finally, in the relationship described between actor and audience, Meyerhold stressed that the audience was manipulated (through a scientific study of reactions) by the actor. Grotowski certainly opposed this, believing that the act of theatre was therapeutic, while for Stanislavski, the unity of art and life was paramount.

In *Drama, Stage, and Audience,* J.L. Styan raises an important point.

> We are so accustomed to seeing actors impersonating "characters" as realistically as possible, trying to the utmost of their bent to convince us of the living actuality of the figures they represent, that we forget that conviction of reality is only one, relatively minor, purpose the actor may pursue. Realism in characterization is so recent an objective for the actor that is does not seem unfair to see it merely a period convention like any other; it is important, but only in so far as it belongs to our time. Realistic acting was a direct result of the naturalistic movement . . . and of the continuing expectations of the film and television media long after the stage had dropped them. As a convention, it has already passed into history because of the greater needs of a succession of dramatic movements from symbolism, expressionism and the absurd, which called for abstract characterization. . . . The actor's role is returning to its former function, which was not first that of impersonation, but nearer to that of interpreter and spokesman.[35]

Although Meyerhold and Grotowski respected, even revered, Stanislavski, they also both rejected the idea that theatre must "realistically" imitate or mirror life. Both rejected naturalism and the naturalistic movement. For Meyerhold, the actor was an interpreter who expressed a dramatic idea through calculated movements and a kinesthetic sense for all that goes on around him. Biomechanics offered a solution to the problem of how this could be achieved. Grotowski was more comfortable with the actor as spokesman, not a spokesman in the interpretive sense, but rather the actor as one who leads the way to removal of the conventions which separate him from the audience. "Grotowski sees the players as one ensemble, the audience as another; when the two are integrated, a play has begun."[36]

To compare and analyze the methods or systems of these men is to question philosophical and theoretical differences which, in the end, offer only more theory. A better comparison for the movement specialist is one which focuses on the particular training aspects of each. What are the benefits that Meyerhold's Biomechanics or Grotowski's "poor theatre" or Stanislavski's method of physical actions offers to actors-in-training, movement specialists, or directors with an interest in stage movement for actors? One benefit is stated by Igor Ilinsky:

An actor does exercises in biomechanics. These exercises were to train us and give us a state for a specific movement onstage. The exercises, partly gymnastic, partly plastic movement, partly acrobatics, were to teach acting students how to calculate their movements; to develop a keen eye, coordinate movements in reference to their partners, and in general give them flexibility so that in future performances the actor could move more freely and expressively in the scenic spaces.[37]

Meyerhold's legacy to modern actors is his Biomechanics system, which reminds the actor of the expressive power of his body, his gestures, and his posture. Just as the mask can create an entire attitude of character, so can the physical, movement style of the actor. Meyerhold often demonstrated this power with the use of puppets. He encouraged the actor to develop a "self-mirror" so that he could know exactly what his body was communicating. According to Ilinsky, Meyerhold is often misread, incorrectly interpreted as having a disregard for the actor's contribution to the total performance. Meyerhold did believe in the power of the actor. He designed his Biomechanical system to aid the actor.

Biomechanics when applied to actor training encourages body strength, flexibility, coordination, and confidence in the physical statement made by the actor. It also gives the actor a sense of "where he is on stage" in relation to other actors, the stage setting, and important objects or props which also inhabit the stage space. A careful study of Biomechanics within the context of rehearsal of a given play offers the actor a better understanding of what could be called his field of vision. Through exercises in the Biomechanical format the actor knows where he is going in his character, both internally and externally. Biomechanics encourages ensemble playing because many of the exercises are developed for actors as they share scenes within the play.

Most importantly, Biomechanics teaches the actor to think about his performance space three-dimensionally. This does not deny the "fourth wall" or mean that actors should not be aware of the audience. In fact, just the opposite occurs. The audience is an accepted part of the theatre experience. It is not ignored. Meyerhold acknowledged the powerful effect an audience can have on a production, its rhythm and timing, its energy, and its overall effect. Biomechanics shows the actor how to calculate and control his movements, timing, and gestures so that all aspects of the performance can be coordinated.

Under Meyerhold's hand the whole of a performance became a
crystallization of meaning. And the code of that meaning, beyond the
language of the text, was *movement—gesture* and the *reaction* that
gesture ineluctably calls forth. Only theatre, by combining language
with patterns of gesture and reaction, can encompass a future....[38]

Like Meyerhold, Grotowski too was interested in the actor's ability
to express emotion through bodily attitudes. He also was interested in
the actor's relationship with the audience.

Although Grotowski's views on theatre and the role theatre plays
in society have changed and evolved since the beginning of the 1980s,
his initial work in the "poor theatre" style has had profound effects on
actor training and the avant-garde movement.

In the preface to the English version of Grotowski's essays, *Towards
a Poor Theatre,* Peter Brook wrote: "Grotowski is unique. Why? Because
no one else in the world, to my knowledge, no one since Stanislavski,
has investigated the nature of acting, its phenomenon, its meaning, the
nature and science of its mental-physical-emotional processes as deeply
and completely as Grotowski. He calls his theatre a laboratory. It is. It
is a centre for research."

Brook, who is himself the most daredevil innovator among theatre
professionals, and the most technical and professional director among
the innovators, knows what he is writing. But applied to the theatre, the
term laboratory is misleading. In a laboratory research, investigation and
tests are conducted. A laboratory can check its methods, but it does not
investigate itself. Theatre-laboratory investigates itself. In this
metaphysics which assumes all appearances of knowledge, the search for
the essence of the theatre is the essence of the theatre.[39]

Grotowski experimented with theatre and the process of making
theatre. He took what most would call "rehearsal," "experiment," or
"investigation" and made it theatre. He probed the illusion of the
theatre reality and made the making of theatre an event. This could be
compared with what Joseph Chaikin called "work in progress." It is,
perhaps, for the contemporary actor, this "work in progress" in the
"poor theatre" style which is most helpful. Grotowski's creative exercises
for the mind, body, and soul can be most enlightening for the actor-in-
training, providing him with a ritualistic and almost spiritual connection with character and text. But the actor-in-performance may face
certain restraints if he chooses to perform in this style. This is not a

mainstream theatre style and most actors are struggling to perform in the mainstream.

Jan Kott reported after observing one of Grotowski's protégés conducting an acting workshop that the student actors were taught to whine, yell, tweet, moan, and scream. Kott cautions that actors should know how to speak before they study how to scream. This raises the question of whether Grotowski's theatre style is of greater benefit in training or in performance. It seems that a study of Grotowski presents a great advantage to the actor-in-training, that is, the actor who is developing creative courage, body flexibility, and ensemble trust. This also includes the actor as he or she works for abstraction or essence of character.

> For Grotowski's actors, the act of creation was by necessity *both* spontaneous and disciplined. In approaching his art, the actor was required to possess "infinite courage"; yet, he was instructed to be prepared at every moment to "resign" himself; he was to be both active and passive. In his exercises, the actor (like the competitive athlete) was required to master the form, the objective elements; at the same time, however, it was important that he impart to these elements the stamp of his subjective self, that he make them *his own*.
>
> Grotowski insisted that the actor's art be one that involved great excesses and equally great austerity. By pushing himself beyond fatigue the actor would enter a state of "passive readiness," a form of alertness indebted, primarily, to fatigue. The body of the actor was subjected to rigorous training so that, according to Grotowski, it might, ultimately, *cease to exist*. And so it went, an unending stream of contradictions—all of which seemed, somehow, to make eminent sense.[40]

If Grotowski approached a contradictory note in his early stage of theatre practice it was, perhaps, because of some key metaphysical concepts which he held to be inviolate. In his interview with Richard Schechner in 1968 Grotowski commented that he had the solution to the questions on acting. He had found the answer to the acting paradox. Yet he then referred to the solutions as "mysterious," and "undefinable."[41]

It is often difficult to explain what happens in therapy and Grotowski's "trance" acting is a kind of theraputic approach to acting, not in the self-analyzing sense so attributed to Lee Strasberg's school of "method" acting, but rather in the deeper sense of true, archetypal psychotherapy. Grotowski's sense of theatre approaches the ritualistic frenzy associated with ancient Greek tragedy. Perhaps in the modern sense he was trying to direct us back to our own rituals so long ago lost in the "richness" of contemporary life.

It is safe to say that all modern theories of acting incorporate some aspect of the Stanislavski System. As Grotowski observed, Stanislavski did ask all of the right questions concerning acting, and although Grotowski and Meyerhold did differ with him, each owed Stanislavski a debt. Stanislavski was the first adequately to develop exercises to encourage the free concentration and manipulation of the mind-body relationship. He recognized the creative state and believed that it could be encouraged and controlled through the use of imagination, relaxation, and most importantly, physical stimulus. Unfortunately, Stanislavski's life ended before he could completely evolve and record his theories. Much of his evolving work was passed down by way of oral tradition, thus offering it to individual interpretations. But as Grigori V. Kristi stated

> he [Stanislavski] cherishes most the spiritual side of creativity but to stir this process within the actor he proposed to begin with the physical nature of the action.[42]

Through Stanislavski's work a bond is established between the spoken text and the physical action. The late twentieth century is an ideal time to combine the best of acting theories into a comprehensive actor training program. This includes the movement aspects of Stanislavski, Meyerhold, and Grotowski's training and performance theory. One can only speculate at the quality of actor training today if these three men were living, working, and influencing one another at the same time.

> ...Meyerhold believed that Biomechanics, based on the study of the actor's body and its reflexes, would make the body an ideal means of expression under the actor's command. (Had these exercises reached America when some of the Stanislavski techniques did, the physical training of our actors would not have been so neglected.)[43]

Biomechanics and the method of physical actions are not to be confused however.

[T]here is an essential difference between these two techniques: Meyerhold thought that certain movements of the highly trained body would stir inner processes within the actor, whereas Stanislavski spoke, not of a movement, but of a purposeful action, which involves the consciousness of the actor. An action is an unbreakable organic psychological process — that is, what the actor thinks, experiences, and does physically in the character's circumstances. (Incidentally, what the Polish director Jerzy Grotowski, who has provoked such interest in the American theatre, perhaps overdramatically calls "the total act" is simply what Stanislavski meant by the complete psychophysical involvement of the actor as the character.) Biomechanics, on the other hand, is based on physical movement only, and thus divides the actor's physical from his psychological behavior. . . . It is an effective discipline for the actor's body, whereas the Method of Physical Actions is Stanislavski's most important contribution to his psychological technique.[44]

But the varied and complex theatre of the post–World War II era demanded a more integrated approach to movement training. Perhaps because of an interest in health and fitness or perhaps due to a new awareness of the fragile nature of the human body, new "body work" was incorporated into actor training.

10. The New Specialists of Movement

[A]cting theorists have come to believe that before an actor can learn to act, to use his bodily instrument expressively in vital characterizations, he must himself learn to move and feel and live anew because in growing up he has disordered his musculature, misshapen his bones, and dulled his sensitivities. The goal at the end of a training program in acting today is natural expressiveness; its enemy is inhibition.[1]

Each era of theatre has had its own proponents of theories which led to an accepted style of theatre. In acting the same has held true since earliest times. Whether the watchword of the day was delivered by Diderot, Stanislavsky, or Grotowski, each has helped to shape and define the acting of his time. Acting theories have been challenged, in fact, some even have been discounted, yet each one has added to the body of knowledge and to the existing realm of acceptability according to taste, style, and convention.

The post–World War II era had as its chief innovator, Jerzy Grotowski. Although many others made significant contributions to the scope and direction of theatre, Grotowski's special interest and experimentation in the areas of actor training and movement have assured him a place in the history of acting.

Today the major new theories in use are accompanying studies in Stanislavski, Meyerhold, or others, and these theories have not been developed by theatre practitioners, but by educators, physical therapists, mind-body specialists, and medical practitioners.

The 1980s were called by some the "me generation." Characterized by many as a selfish, consumer-obsessed generation, those living during the 1980s were bombarded with products of a new society. By 1990 the Western world, particularly the United States, had become a high-tech, computer regulated society in which every aspect of life has been opened for study, probing, and reporting. This life style has surely influenced the theatre and methods of actor training.

It appears that the major fear for contemporary actors is that they have lost touch with their bodies. The connection between mind (emotion), body (physicalization), and impulse (connection and spontaneity) have been lost in the fast-paced, stressed lives characteristic of the present era. For this reason much of the major concentration in actor training during the late 1970s and early 1980s focused on, or included, the body integration and movement theories of Moshe Feldenkrais, F.M. Alexander, and Rudolf Laban. Although these three men are only representatives of a number of body/movement specialists whose theories are studied, they do pose the most significant and widely used systems of today.

In addition to Alexander Technique, Laban Effort/Shape, and Feldenkrais' Body Awareness, a number of other systems, theories and programs have emerged over the past two decades. These include work associated with and incorporating specific techniques from t'ai chi and t'ai kuan Do, modern dance (Erick Hawkins, Hanya Holm, and Alwin Nikolais technique primarily), yoga, and most recently Alexander Lowen's Bioenergetic exercises, Reiki, and neurolinguistic work. These last programs represent the cutting edge of movement training for the actor and will be described later in this chapter.

The works of Feldenkrais, Alexander, and Laban are in widespread use in the actor training programs around the United States and each has been in existence long enough for its rewards and benefits to have been proven. Alexander Technique and Feldenkrais' Body Integration are included in training programs in many college and university theatre degree plans, as well as in many regional and resident theatre companies. Laban's Effort/Shape has been studied quite extensively in theatre programs in Britain as well as the United States.

Specifically, the Alexander Technique has been used in segments of acting and movement classes at the Dallas Theatre Center's graduate program in connection with Trinity University in San Antonio. Laban's Effort/Shape comprised the entire foundation of the movement classes taught there until 1984 when it severed its ties with Trinity University. Undergraduate as well as graduate students at Southern Methodist's Meadows School of the Arts in Dallas use Alexander Technique extensively in their actor training program. The Meadows School also utilizes Feldenkrais, period movement, and Todd's Body Mechanics.

The American Repertory Theatre Institute for Advanced Theatre Training at Harvard University requires four semesters of movement. Their program is comprised of yoga, dance, akido, and the Tomaschevski mime technique.

The American Conservatory Theatre in San Francisco offers one of the most extensive movement training programs in the United States. Movement courses in the three year program include modern dance and ballet, stage and period movement, yoga, fencing, combat, and Alexander Technique. The Alexander Technique sessions meet for twenty weeks, one and one-half hour per week during the first year, with one half hour weekly individual sessions the second year.

The Lee Strasberg Theatre Institute in New York offers dance classes which encompass aspects of Laban's Effort/Shape. The Institute also offers t'ai chi to integrate the actor's body organically.

These are only a few representative programs from the United States which offer a variety of movement methods for the actor. The programs suggested by Feldenkrais, Alexander, and Laban are by far the most widely used in acting schools today.

These three theorists have had widespread influence on current actor training programs, specifically on movement training and body awareness.

Moshe Feldenkrais worked with children and adults, the terminally ill, the crippled, the over-stressed and the psychotic, as well as the artist and the actor. He proclaimed a reeducation of the body through the discipline he developed after a soccer injury which affected his knees. This sports injury, it would seem, changed the direction of his life and inspired him to investigate a whole system of the mind-body relationship. Feldenkrais was, until his death, the director of the Feldenkrais Institute in Tel Aviv and the author of sixteen books, including *Awareness Through Movement, Body and Mature Behavior,* and *The Potent Self.*

Feldenkrais held a doctorate in physics from the Sorbonne and worked in that field until he was fifty. Perhaps it was his background in science which led him to study so energetically after an injury to his knee. Already accomplished at yoga and judo, after his knee injury he became interested in studies in anatomy and physiology, biochemistry, and neurophysiology.[2] He was given little hope of a full recovery from physicians, so he set out to cure himself. The results must have been remarkable for soon thereafter he began consulting with friends possessed of a variety of complaints. His method of bodily integration, health, and energy evolved.

Feldenkrais' work began to appear in the United States in the early 1970s. By the mid 1980s there were over a hundred training centers in the United States and Israel from which trained practitioners held workshops and seminars.

> Students of all ages come from widely different backgrounds. The teacher does not demonstrate the movement or make physical corrections during class but instead gives verbal directions and descriptions. Each person works to achieve the goals of the lesson as fully as his body permits. He follows his own time and makes his own choices about how best to organize the limbs and the torso to do what the teacher describes.[3]

Feldenkrais' therapeutic work can be divided into two branches: the group oriented sessions of "Awareness Through Movement," and the one-to-one sessions of "Functional Integration." According to Feldenkrais' theory, the body finds its own way back to its optimum position, posture, or confirmation. A new stance or way of moving is never imposed on the body. No rules of movement exist in the Feldenkrais method, but rather each body must seek its own path to integration. Often the student may not realize changes are occurring until he or she is asked to walk about and move freely. Much of the work in "Awareness Through Movement" takes place on the floor. The student lies prone and may be asked to roll from side to side with knees pulled up or with legs extended. Emphasis is always on the ease of the movement. Whether actions are performed while lying, standing, or moving, smoothness, ease, and naturalness are the goals.

Feldenkrais believed that the integration of major body quadrants and hence, the joints, has been broken by "educational systems and cultural pressures."[4] Society, according to Feldenkrais, is responsible for the betrayal of the body. Modern society demands competition in order for its members to succeed. Modern man is seduced into the idea that successful competition can provide uniqueness and a sense of self esteem while at the same time conformity is the rule for acceptance. Competition shapes us into what we should be; conformity locks us into sameness. The two are incompatible and hence, Feldenkrais believed that the normal growth of humans was suppressed.

No doubt the stress and strain of contemporary life invite chronic muscle problems which lead to emotional problems as well. Feldenkrais believed that the contemporary adult has grown up with a series of negative educational stimuli. He cites forcing children to walk or talk too early, poor posture based on so-called "correct" and stylish posture, traditional physical education, and emotional tensions connected to and a predictable outcome of the physical problems. By the time the adult is aware of his state of being, he has restricted breathing, arthritic joints, inflexible spines, and chronic muscular pain. Perhaps the greatest tragedy, according to Feldenkrais, is the manner in which most accept this fate. His system sets out to change our body concept, our body posture, and our body motor functions.

Feldenkrais and his fellow practitioners prefer the term reeducation when referring to the changes brought about in their clients. The term implies that negative habits or modes of behavior have been carefully, if unconsciously, learned and can, therefore, be unlearned. Once the negative is unlearned, however, a new system must be introduced, hence the reeducation of the body. The approach includes:

1) drawing on early developmental patterns of human mobility; 2) providing more accurate data on spatial relationships of the parts of the body; 3) bringing habitual motor patterns to conscious attention; 4) developing a more articulate spine; and 5) establishing more organic breathing patterns, which make greater lung capacity available and free the rib cage and upper torso.

Feldenkrais' lesson also engages students in making a more accurate assessment of their bodies in space: how the limbs lie as they rest on the floor; whether the parts are symmetrical or asymmetrical; and how the energy flows between them. The goal is to help each individual establish a more complete body image or "schema" and more sensitive kinesthetic responses which Feldenkrais sees as leading to a richer sense of self.[5]

Throughout all of the reeducation process, emphasis is placed on concentration and attention to the exercises, even to minute detail.

Many students state an immediate and surprising change in their body movements and kinesthetic awareness. According to M. Myers, a participant in an "Awareness Through Movement" lesson guided by Norma Leitiko, many students become more "grounded" and move with much more ease after only one or two lessons. Myers attributes this change, in part, to the relaxed manner in which the movements are executed and to the use of repetition of each movement. The method seems so simple yet conclusive that some are, at first, suspicious of it. As Myers states, "Feldenkrais lessons are neurologically sneaky."[6] According to Feldenkrais the body will seek its own path to health if given the proper opportunity. The reeducation provides for that opportunity exclusive of tension, patterned behavior, and body ignorance.

While much of Moshe Feldenkrais' work in body awareness and integration has been therapeutic in its direction, his views have found their way into the studio and use by actors-in-training. For some he may be faith healer, quack, clinician, or guru. For others his work has represented a profound change in the way in which they live, move, and feel. For the most part Feldenkrais sought a health maintenance program which could serve as an alternative to drug therapy, hospitalization, or resignation to a life of diminishing abilities. For theatre practitioners his work represented a new point of view on a long-standing question, What is the relationship of mind to the body and can it be controlled? From Feldenkrais' point of view not only was there a definite relationship between mind and body, but one which could be strengthened. As M. Myers states in an article in *Dance Magazine,*

> I recalled Moshe Feldenkrais' insistence on the unity of mind and body, and the arguments he draws from various scientific disciplines to support his conclusion that thought, emotion, and sensation do not occur without corresponding changes in the muscles of the body and, vice versa, changes in the interrelation of muscle patterns can activate and alter attitudes, thoughts, and feelings.[7]

Although Feldenkrais never refers to Diderot in his writings, it seems, theoretically at least, that there is agreement in principle. For Diderot was the first to establish firmly the relationship between psychological drive and physical response. Feldenkrais had the same idea and he posed a system of exercises which could allow for greater freedom of movement and a stronger connection between the physical characterization and the internal stimuli.

The potential of the use of Feldenkrais' "Awareness Through Movement" or "Body Integration" for the actor-in-training lies in the opportunity for the actor to develop a more flexible and responsive body. Actors, like others in a variety of walks of life, experience the same stresses, negative conditioning and chronic muscular problems. The results of these life patterns can be especially devastating for the actor, for his livelihood can be affected. If an actor has an unresponsive body the quality of his performance may be severely limited. Feldenkrais poses through awareness and integration not only a body which is more supple, flexible, and strong, but one which is capable of reacting to internal stimuli with great sensitivity.

In all of Feldenkrais' exercises he stresses ease, enjoyment, and slowness. In actor training the Feldenkrais method is most advantageous when performed in conjunction with exercises or improvisations based on characterization or text. That is, of course, unless the actors are working on their personal body problems and not those connected with character interpretations. In *The Master Moves*, based on transcripts from Feldenkrais seminars, Chapter Twelve outlines the different aspects or "centers" of focus on body awareness. Included among them are "Thinking and Doing," "Exploring the Floor: The Movements of the Shoulder," "The Ribs and Rolling," "Arm Circles," "The Movement of the Eye Organizes the Movement of the Body," "Jaw, Tongue and Aggression," and "Learning to Sit from Lying."

Each small segment of movement is analyzed and repeated in its most simple form. These types of exercises are very useful for the actor and correspond with much of the physicalization work proposed by Stanislavski.

Feldenkrais' work is utilized by many dancers as well as by actors. Ironically,

> Dancers sometimes have more difficulty than nondancers in achieving a flow of energy from one body part to another because, in their training, they have learned to hold the rib cage, press down the shoulders, or keep the lower back rigid and buttocks contracted.[8]

Feldenkrais' approach is ideal for actors because, at the same time they are working on "reeducating" the body to a more natural manner of moving, they are developing sensory awareness. Feldenkrais' method allows for development of "zero position." Zero position is a term which describes proper body alignment in a relaxed state. Zero position also denotes an absence of personal movement clichés, idiosyncratic ways of standing or tension in a particular part of the body. This position is an advantageous, relaxed but energetic starting point for the actor. Zero position also frees the mind from distractions, thus allowing for better concentration. Feldenkrais' method dispels the problem described by Jean Sabatine in *The Actor's Image:*

> Unless our attention is forcefully called to what is slovenly in our posture or carriage, we remain blissfully ignorant of our distortions.
> For an actor, such problems spell professional disaster; he drags his misshapen image into every characterization, and unless his bad habits happen to be extraordinarily captivating, leading into a career as a popular single type character actor, his professional opportunities to drag himself into characterizations are likely to be severely limited.[9]

Through his simple and gentle exercises Moshe Feldenkrais offers a positive component in the movement training of the actor. Through proper body alignment, conscious awareness of the body and how it moves through time and space, and the relationship of mind to body, the actor can free himself to greater depths and variety of characterization. The creative spirit can be unleashed when the body acts and reacts sensitively.

Most of Feldenkrais' exercises and theories on movement are not new to theatre movement practitioners. The imagery used in his exercises is reflective of Stanislavski; the mind-body relationship is parallel to Diderot. The simplicity and ease of movement are congruent with F.M. Alexander, yoga, and much of what is held true by body practitioners.

> The Alexander Technique is a means of developing integration of the body and mind in action through the re-education of kinesthetic perceptions. This process offers a positive experience of self—as light, expansive, flowing and harmonious—leading to dynamic balance, coordination, and alignment. A pioneer in the field of mind/body

integration, the Alexander Technique helps performers become attuned to themselves and others on a subtle yet highly energized level of organization.[10]

The use of Alexander Technique as developed by F. Matthais Alexander (1869–1955) is today even more widespread in actor training programs and theatre companies than the work of Feldenkrais. Today the Alexander Technique is used in such programs as the Juilliard School, the American Conservatory Theatre, and the American Shakespeare Festival. F. Matthais Alexander first developed his technique in the late 1890s. Like Feldenkrais, Alexander believed in mind-body integration as a means through which the body could exist as an harmonious organism. While Feldenkrais referred to "body integration" Alexander's watchword for the same concept was "divine neutral." "When performers can come to a 'divine neutral,' a state in which the self is well balanced, flexible, and adaptable — they can become clear channels for the ideas they wish to express."[11]

Emphasis is placed on proper body alignment (posture), proper breath control, and effective movement patterns which are carefully analyzed by the conscious awareness of the student. The Alexander Technique is an effective tool for the actor seeking to improve his body and bodily characterizations as well as his voice. Alexander acknowledged that positive vocal control can only work in conjunction with positive body mechanics.

The Alexander Technique is a popular method of body awareness training among actors because it lends itself so well to the arena of actors preparing characterizations. Alexander and his followers have made a concerted effort to include the technique in training programs in addition to its clinical uses. According to Aileen Crow, director of her own school for Alexander Technique in New York,

> Through the Alexander Technique performers can release fixed tension patterns, leaving themselves open to assume many different body attitudes and breathing patterns, and to play those characters who are ecstatic, victimized, ingratiating, compassionate, "correct," or condescending. . . . These physical attitudes then become material for the creative process, to be worn by choice and with conscious skill.[12]

The Alexander Technique focuses on proper body alignment and conscious awareness of movement patterns, but great emphasis is also placed on proper breathing, which Alexander felt was at the center of all good movement. He discovered the importance of good breathing after suffering the loss of his voice several times during his career as an actor. He noted a definite relation between breathing and the result of the force of gravity on the body's posture. In addition, Alexander found that most people use the forces of gravity and inertia most ineffectively, that is, instead of allowing these natural laws of physics to work *for* the body, most people work against these forces, thus actually creating more work and tension for themselves.

Sarah Barker, an Alexander Technique instructor, explains the secret which Alexander discovered.

> That secret is a small but perceptible contraction of the muscles at the back of his neck, and it precedes all efforts at vocal articulation.... He must release that contraction with movement of his head upward.
>
> Basically, the action that most often precedes wasteful or harmful responses is a contraction which pulls the head slightly backward and down. The effect of this is a compression of the spine, which, repeated hundreds of times a day over a span of many years, interferes with the smooth operation of the muscular and nervous systems of all the vital organs.
>
> And this is only *one* destructive habit, the first of a whole series that will follow if the first occurs unchallenged. Taken together, this destructive series can compress the body's trunk, thus squeezing the delicate organs that reside there, reducing lung capacity and projecting the stomach unpleasingly forward. It can lead to round-the-clock tension in some muscles, which can cause loss of voice, high blood pressure and chronic joint and muscle pains.
>
> To eliminate the problem at its source, we need to prevent the neck from contracting unnecessarily. And doing this means using the conscious mind to change our *sub*conscious muscle patterns. In order to revise things of which we are not aware, we need a new approach — one that can bring subconscious sensations forward into the conscious mind. With every act, we can consciously move our head upward, body following it.[13]

While practicing the Alexander Technique, whether one-to-one or in group sessions, an extremely light, almost feather-like touch is used by the instructor. The instructor anticipates movement in the student and guides the muscles or muscle groups in a more healthy direction. Considerable time and attention are given to freeing the neck and head so that the head rides easily and effortlessly on top of the neck and upper body, lengthening the spine, expanding the shoulders and upper rib cage, balancing the pelvis, and freeing the legs so that they may move freely, thus supporting the torso and upper body, but not laboring under the weight of such.

These aspects of body therapy allow for the student to replace through conscious control a poor body habit (any learned inefficient movement) with a more productive body habit. In the Alexander Technique, a mental activity is responsible for replacing the negative with the positive. "Alexander believed that people can learn to inhibit an inefficient movement pattern and consciously substitute one that produces more harmonious movement and feelings of ease and well-being."[14]

Alexander chose the word "use" to describe what his technique could provide.

> Good use means moving the body with maximum balance and coordination of all parts so that only the effort absolutely needed is expended. Bad use means employing the body in a haphazard way: one part of the body compensates at random, and usually inefficiently, for the movement of another in order to maintain balance and stability. Good or bad, however, everything we do in life manifests itself in the way we "use" ourselves.
>
> Through the Alexander Technique, you learn instead one Basic Movement that can control the normal flow of all your activity. The aim of the Technique is to allow a condition of ease throughout the body without creating any new distortions in the process.[15]

Alexander Technique, like Feldenkrais' method, has been used in dance training as well as actor training. Alexander, for the dancer, is usually turned to after an injury or because of some chronic physical problem. Alexander, in most cases, is used only with an instructor or trainer. It is an on-going therapy, not a technique to be learned and then forgotten. One must constantly and consciously practice the "three basic steps of the technique: awareness of a movement pattern, inhibition of that pattern, and substitution of a new one."[16]

In the early steps of an Alexander Technique session much of the work is done while the student is seated. The trainer gently, with feather touch of the index and middle fingers, strokes the muscles of the neck and head, inviting a more relaxed state and longer extension of the back of the head. There is no pushing or manipulating, but rather the technique might best be described as "feeling."

Usually the results are quite dramatic, but not necessarily long-standing. First the student must become aware of the changes in progress. Mirrors are of invaluable use so that the student might see the physical changes as they occur. Once the head, neck, and spine have been lengthened, the shoulders are directed open and out with the firm but gentle use of the palms of the hands of the trainer. Through a gentle rocking method and with conscious awareness of the breathing, the student rises or "rolls" out of his seat and begins to walk and move about. Usually there is a feeling of "floating" or walking on "air" as the student first experiences the sensation of moving up and out of his pelvis. Work on the legs and knees often begins while the student is reclining.

> [T]here is no standard of exercises, physical movements, or practices in the Alexander Technique. The emphasis is rather on a state of mind and a way of doing that involves a continually renewed willingness not to achieve any results. For Alexander, the emphasis lies on the "means whereby" rather than on the "end-gaining."[17]

In *The Alexander Technique* Sarah Barker outlines nine rules to follow when applying the Alexander Technique to oneself outside the aid of a trainer. Many of the exercises are similar to those which are used in the training sessions. She suggests that students consider the head to mean the entire head and not only the face or chin. Emphasis is placed on awareness of the top of the head as the end extension of the spine. Body refers to the entire torso and it must move as though it were connected to the legs and arms. The student is reminded to think of the body moving in an "upward" direction so that the force of gravity does not pull the movements down.

The "Basic Movement" is an action which should be repeated so that the student can "check in" with how the body is moving. The "Basic Movement" is an action of turning the head and focusing on different points in the room. Action or exercises are not performed at any particular pace, the student must find the pace which is best for him at that time. Students are reminded always to be aware of the breathing. The breathing is the key to alive and energetic body use. All movement should be executed with flexibility and freedom as its key. The "correct" way for one would not necessarily be the "correct" way for someone else. Breathing should be done through the nose. Actions should be done with a sense of spontaneity. Movement habits can lead to poor body usage.[18]

The Alexander Technique provides a system of reeducation by which the actor may gain greater control over his physical and connected emotional abilities which must be used in characterizations. The actor is freed from old habits which probably restrain him both mentally and physically. Alexander and Feldenkrais would agree that for every action in the physical body (a release or acquisition of a tension, for example) there is a corresponding reaction. Also, anything which profoundly affects the body will surely affect the mind as well. These conclusions are paramount if contemporary actors are to be able to meet the needs of the contemporary theatre.

> [T]o study movement is to study man, for movement is both the medium and the vehicle for all kinds of human activity and a deeper understanding and a heightened awareness of movement can bring a greater richness to life.[19]

Rudolf von Laban (1879–1958) was a Hungarian-born scholar, teacher, movement specialist, lecturer, and student of mankind. He was fascinated by all aspects of the human experience; the personality, the behavior, the psychology, and especially, human movement. He wrote in *The Mastery of Movement*, "man moves to satisfy a need. He aims1 his movements towards something of value to him."[20] During his life he studied dance, painting, architecture, and ancient rituals in an effort to gain greater understanding of contemporary men and women.

Like others before him, Laban worked with a wide variety of people in many different situations before coming to his own conclusions about human movement and its potential effects on our lives and our relationships. He studied worker's movement patterns, he worked with sick and disabled children and adults, and he explored the relationship between creative artists and their movements. He is most widely recognized for the development of his kinesthetic shorthand or Labanotation. This shorthand or notation system allowed for a precise description of human movement to be recorded and studied later.

> The development of a simple, quickly written "shorthand" of movement meant that it was possible to capture and record how a person moves. Before the symbols could be invented, it was necessary to understand how to look at movement itself, and still today this is the biggest hurdle for a student observer.[21]

Labanotation was only one aspect of Laban's research into human movement. He also developed the study of *choreutics*, "The practical study of the various forms of more or less harmonized movement."[22] Although much of the results of his research were used by managers and workers to better utilize time and labor and to battle worker's fatigue, his greatest contributions were in the areas of dance and actor training.

> Beginning in the first years of the present century, he worked on experiments exploring the nature of human movement, and on a systematic analysis of so-called plastic rhythm. As early as 1910, in Munich, his first movement-choirs performed dancing for recreation. He was successful in developing huge civic festivals; throughout his life, he was concerned with the nature of work movements and the effective utilization of effort in labor. After directing his own dance company, which performed a number of experimental works, Laban became Ballet Master of the State Theatre in Berlin during the 1920s. However, his most notable work was not in choreography, but in terms of his analysis of the physical laws governing dance movement, and the approach to dance training that he developed with his pupil and collaborator, Kurt Jooss.[23]

Laban found that human movement could be analyzed and described from one or both of two points of view. One, the spatial patterns of movements — that is, how the body moves through space or how the extremities move in relation to the torso; and two, in terms of the rhythm of the movement. This latter description he called "effort" and it was this effort theory which was of most interest to actors.

Laban believed that movement was expressive of all of human desires, both conscious and unconscious. Movement, therefore, was always performed for a reason. This connection between the inner motivation and the outer manifestation of movement allowed for the actor to gain a direct link to the character's inner intentions and outer posture, gesture vocabulary, and entire movement confirmation. As Samuel Thornton states in *Laban's Theory of Movement,*

> Movement is not the mere motion of limbs and body in some haphazard way divorced from inner participation; it is the visible manifestation of man's true intellectual, emotional and spiritual state. . . . It is the link between man's intentions and their realization through action. This link, between the covert and the overt behaviour of man, Laban termed the *flow of movement*. . . .[24]

It is the effort which gives way to the flow of movement. The efforts are made up of four movement factors: space, weight, time, and flow. That is to say that all movements occur in some direction (straight or curved) through space; they are executed with some resistance or acceptance of weight (heavy movements or light movements); they are performed either fast or slow; and each movement pursues some succession of flow. "Effort is involved in every voluntary and involuntary movement; therefore to understand movement it is necessary to comprehend the effort life of man."[25]

Laban named each basic effort according to the four movement factors

Light	Heavy
Flick (fast, curved)	Slash (fast, curved)
Float (slow, curved)	Wring (slow, curved)
Glide (slow, straight)	Press (slow, straight)
Dab (fast, straight)	Punch (fast, straight)[26]

Although the titles of each effort quality may appear to be an arbitrary description of the movement itself, the effort concept can offer the actor a helpful movement vocabulary on which to base a character study, and more importantly, on which to base the relationship between movement and inner feelings.

[E]ffort is manifested in bodily actions through Weight, Time, Space, Flow elements. Not all of these motion factors are always significant and according to their combination they produce particular shading.

Whilst animals' movements are instinctive and mainly done in response to external stimuli, those of man are charged with human qualities and he expresses himself and communicates through his movements something of his inner being. He has the faculty of becoming aware of the patterns which his effort impulses create and of learning to develop, to re-shape and to use them.

The actor, the dancer, the mime whose job it is to convey thoughts, feelings and experiences through bodily actions, has not only to master these patterns but also to understand their significance. In this way imagination is enriched and expression developed.[27]

Laban believed that movement was the essence of the actor's material and a deeper understanding of movement could provide an invaluable link between actor and character. When the effort concept is used by actors-in-training, the movement factors are first studied in isolation. For example, the actor may execute individual studies in float, glide, or dab. The actor explores the kinesthetic space around his own body through movement factors of a specific time, weight, or direction in space. Once the actor has a working knowledge of each movement factor or effort in its abstracted, isolated form, he then can work to combine efforts or use them in more realistic improvisations. Through the use of improvisations and the use of realistic "work actions" (glide is the same action used while ironing, wring is the action used in wringing out wet clothes, and dab is the same action as typing) the actor could develop a movement improvisation for the character. Laban also combined the efforts with spoken words.

Examples of the movements of everyday working actions that can be applied to the expression of inner states of mind and emotion are legion, but there exist a few such as pressing, thrusting, wringing, slashing, gliding, dabbing, flicking, and floating which are the basic actions of a working person, and, at the same time, the fundamental movements of emotional and mental expression. Sounds and words are formed by movements of the speech organs, and these are rooted in the same basic actions. Sounds can be produced, by pressing, thrusting or other movements of the speech organs, and will result in pressing and thrusting accents of the words. Such accents are expressive of the inner mood of the speaker.[28]

In one particular exercise described in *The Mastery of Movement* Laban suggests that the actor repeat the simple word "no" with the different shades of meanings of the efforts.[29] Through careful repetition of such an exercise Laban believed that actors could broaden their verbal mastery of sound qualities and expressive abilities. This could be carried even into movement expression as well. Laban held that an actor, like a musician, must learn to develop a skill for memorizing a score. The score inside the actor's memory was not one of musical notes, but rather movement expressions. This "score" could be repeated at will by the trained and experienced actor.

Laban cautions the actor against becoming too specialized in one direction of his study. A study of movement should open and free the actor, not restrict him within a particular aspect of development. Laban states:

> The best way to acquire and develop the capacity of using movement as a means of expression on the stage is to perform simple movement scenes. First the student should become fully conscious of the character of the person to be represented, the kind of values after which he or she strives, and the circumstances in which the striving occurs. Then, as a part of his creative function as a performing artist, he must select the movements appropriate to the character, the values, and the particular situation. This selection involves intensive work. Improvisation of the acted scene, however brilliant, is not enough, nor is it sufficient to memorize a seemingly effective movement combination.[30]

Laban believed that performance of character portrayal was a synthesis of the actor's mental and physical attributes with both movement and sound (vocal) personifications growing naturally, if not easily, out of uninhibited creative work. Movement, he believed, was the essence and truth of the work.

Efforts, which are the link between the mental and the physical, are similar to the mind-body connection of which Feldenkrais wrote and the body awareness concepts of Alexander. Laban chose to classify movement, to develop an alphabet or vocabulary through which the component factors of movement (or mind-body relationship) might be described.

In *Mastery of Movement* Laban outlines several improvisational scenes for the actor-in-training to rehearse and perform in order to develop better movement awareness and movement sensitivity. In one particular exercise the actor performs a scene of emotion, such as love, passion, pain, or hate. The actor must analyze the efforts, experiment with different ways of conveying the emotion and, finally, try to impose a different rhythm on the scene. Different rhythms may affect different characters in a variety of ways. Other improvisations include scenes of practical actions (without props), scenes of period movement (body carriage), and scenes of unusual surroundings.[31]

Unlike the credo of some "method actors" that honesty of emotion is all that is necessary, Laban felt that certain artistic choices must be weighed and made before the performance could be called significant. A dramatic work, like a musical or dance performance, must be "composed into a whole, if an effective work of stagecraft is to be built up."[32] The point is to create a work with a particular point of view, one with a unique statement on life or some aspect of life, not merely a representation of everyday events. It is for this reason that Laban believed the actor should analyze and understand the significance of human movement in the deepest sense. This differs from an appreciation of movement and an ability to reproduce pantomimically.

The theatre trends and practices of the 1960s were varied, complex, and in many cases experimental. Such performance groups as the Living Theatre, the Bread and Puppet Theatre, Grotowski's Polish Lab Theatre, the Open Theatre, and Happenings changed our expectations concerning traditional acting and theatre. The needs and directions of movement were pushed to their limits.

Intuitively, the underground theatre of the 1960s and 1970s was a theatre of movement and gesture. This theatre was a kaleidoscope of traditions, some from the Orient, some from a combination of the visual arts, dance, music, and theatre, still others from dreams, politics, collective movements, and pure improvisation. Just as the performances themselves turned inward, so did the means through which the actors prepared themselves for such performances—or nonperformances. It was during this time that the ancient arts of t'ai chi and t'ai chuan were first utilized by actors in movement training. Yoga, fencing, stage combat, and period dance had long been included in movement training.

During the late 1970s new theories on movement appeared from the holistic, guide-to-energy, health, and rejuvenation concepts. Actors borrowed from these concepts in an effort to integrate mind, body, health, awareness, and energy focus. These techniques are experimental and time will tell if they are truly beneficial for the actor's needs.

> Reiki is a powerful yet gentle, subtle yet precise art and science of restoring your depleted energy and of balancing natural energy within you to promote healing, positive wellness, wholeness, consciousness, and ultimately, enlightenment. . . . It is a natural energy-activating method. It is a precise way of using "light-energy" to restore and balance your own vital energy — physically, emotionally, and mentally — and to connect with your inner self — your spirit.[33]

Barbara Weber Ray is a trainer in Reiki and is founder of the American Reiki Association, Inc. Reiki's main aim is healing and wellness through a control of personal energy which resists negative impulses. An Oriental healing art, *ki* is Chinese for basic life-force. Reiki invites a harmony of mind and body. Certain life factors like stress, food, and environmental conditions can affect this harmony, thus allowing for disharmony and a disruption of the life force. Reiki is a precise system which can be learned for self-use. Students can learn to control their own "life-force" or energy. Reiki masters or trainers must complete three degrees of Reiki instruction. Dr. Ray equates these three degrees with the B.A. (First Degree Reiki), the M.A. (Second Degree Reiki), and the Ph.D. (Third Degree Reiki).

> The Reiki technique applies natural vital energy in a systematic treatment to your body. In brief, the treatment begins at the top of the head and in four steps covers the eyes, the sinus tracts, the brain, the pituitary and pineal glands, the throat, and the thyroid gland. In this step, all anatomy from the neck up is treated. In the next four steps, the lungs, heart, liver, gall-bladder, stomach, spleen, pancreas, intestines, bladder, and reproductive organs are treated thoroughly. There are four steps for covering your back, which include the heart, lungs, adrenal glands, kidneys, spinal cord, lower back, and intestines. In the Reiki Seminar, complete details are given regarding this treatment and the use of Reiki with specific diseases and/or as a health and wholeness maintenance technique.[34]

Bioenergetics is a dual focused technique. First, it "is a way of understanding personality in terms of the body and its energetic processes."[35] Bioenergetics is also a therapeutic process which combines the mind and body in an effort to resolve problems and assure a more healthful and happier life. "The fundamental thesis of bioenergetics is that body and mind are functionally identical: that is what goes on in the mind reflects what is happening in the body and vice versa."[36]

Bioenergetics presupposes that the mind and body influence one another on a conscious level while at the same time, on an unconscious level, the processes of thinking and feeling are influenced by energy factors. Bioenergetics is useful for relieving stress, depression, and anxiety. For the actor, it provides sensory awareness, energy control, control of nervousness, and focus control. The program of Bioenergetics includes "manipulative procedures" and mental and physical exercises.

> The manipulative procedures consist of massage, controlled pressure, and gentle touching to relax contracted muscles. The exercises are designed to help a person get in touch with his tensions and relax them through appropriate movement.[37]

The physical exercises include stretching, flexing, arching, and breathing exercises. Alexander Lowen, a practicing psychiatrist, outlines the benefits of Bioenergetics as

1. Increasing the energy state of the body,
2. Grounding or centering the torso in the legs and body.
3. Deepening the breathing and benefits of effective respiration.
4. Increasing self awareness; and
5. Increasing self-expression and confidence.

Alexander Lowen is quick to state that Bioenergetics is a form of therapy and the benefits of it cannot be realized unless the exercises are sincerely and deliberately performed. Movement trainers have borrowed much from the Bioenergetics program, not so much for a therapeutic need, but because the exercises are designed to relieve tension and the program relates the mind and body so effectively together.

The difficult and long process of training the actor has, during the twentieth century, finally focused attention on the art of stage movement. Much of this attention came about because actors were called upon to portray characters in a more natural and realistic style and the physical demands on the actor were increasing. Those who first drew attention were movement specialists, not actors, directors, or even choreographers. Many who have added the most to our current view on movement for the stage were therapists, not artists. Such is the case with Feldenkrais, Alexander, and Laban.

Each of these men was involved in a search for meaning in movement and a connection between human movement and human behavior. Feldenkrais and Alexander both believed that the stresses of modern society have caused people to lose touch with their bodies. Because they have lost this connection they are no longer integrated beings. Through their work these three individuals hope to reestablish this integration—with different methods, of course, but with the same ultimate goal. Laban's interest in human movement did not begin out of a therapeutic need but rather out of a desire to systematize movement so that it could be analyzed, interpreted, and understood. Nonetheless, each of these has contributed to the progress of movement training for the actor, especially in the years since World War II.

The work of Feldenkrais and Alexander is most valuable to the actor-in-training and to movement training programs because of its basic therapeutic thrust. Actors, who fall victim to the stresses, injuries, and maladies of all mortals, have had no source from which to gain help prior to the lessons advocated by "Awareness Through Movement" and the "divine neutral." Actors in the past have been forced to consult orthopedists, chiropractors, dance teachers, or physical education coaches to obtain help in their unique physical problems, either creative or physiological. Practitioners well versed in the teachings of Feldenkrais and Alexander have been able to solve some of these problems and with the particular needs of the theatre artist in mind.

A study of stage movement presents a peculiar problem to the actor and the coach or teacher, for it is only recently that this area of study has been given a proper place in the total actor training program.

11. The Future of Movement Training

The use of movement in acting enables the actor to communicate far more than the spoken words of the playwright. The same is true in life. Albert Mehrabian is one of many who have stated that nonverbal, or movement, signals are more powerful in their expressive capacity than the words we use. According to Mehrabian only 7 percent of meaning is communicated by words; 38 percent is by the voice, its tone and inflection, and 55 percent is by nonverbal means, or facial expressions, gestures, posture, touch, an so on. "A great many forms of nonverbal behavior can communicate feeling...."[1] It is evident that humans in everyday life, as well as actors in a play, can communicate much more with their bodily attitudes and actions than they do with words. These nonverbal signals may communicate in subtle and unconscious ways. We are not always aware of the signals we send or receive, yet they are powerful and revealing. Many people live out their lives without much thought as to what is expressed or how often we concentrate more on the spoken word, tone of voice, pronunciation, or voice quality. When we do communicate ineffectively, it is difficult to find the cause or the solution. Still, few have access to systems which can improve their communication and few seek out the systems available. Communication is taken for granted. We speak, we move, we cry, shout, embrace, and play. Unless some organic problem arises or our lives are disrupted by crises in our relationships, we proceed as we have in the past.

The actor is not afforded this attitude towards communication. He cannot take any element of his dramatic communication for granted.

Certainly, all aspects of the vocal presentation are important. In *Physical Movement for the Theatre,* Peter Kline and Nancy Meadows state:

> Few actors take the fullest advantage of their opportunity to communicate. Since more than half of the message is conveyed by the body, it is extremely important that the actor make his body as subtle and expressive in movement as possible.[2]

I have attempted to describe attitudes towards movement for the actor in an historical context for the purpose of providing a backdrop against which changes in these attitudes took place. Significant changes have taken place from antiquity to the present concerning theories of acting and the importance of the actor's physical presence. This book focuses only in part on the history of movement training. An historical sense of how movement has been used and the actor's training in movement is vital. Much of our experience is based on cumulative knowledge in this area. In addition it is important to understand past attitudes toward the actor's physical presence so that when producing historical or period productions we may perform them more accurately.

The theatre of the twentieth century is complex. It is representative of a complex and varied age and a myriad of styles and genres are included. Attitudes toward acting have changed significantly over the ages and these alterations have occurred more rapidly since the mid-nineteenth century. In a struggle to define acting in the twentieth century it has been said that:

> acting is being; acting is believing; acting is feeling; acting is doing; acting is becoming; acting is illusion; acting is technique; acting is instinct; acting is craft; acting is creative; acting is reacting; acting is rehearsing; acting is game....[3]

Certainly all of these are true. This wide-range definition echoes an important change from the past when acting was considered to be exhibition or imitation.

The innovations in acting and stage movement have been heralded by the performance theories of Stanislavski and Grotowski. Meyerhold has been included because of his Biomechanics system for actor training—a system which can now be studied in more depth partly because of relaxed attitudes by the Soviet Union and the new translations of his work. Much of the work outlined in Meyerhold's Biomechanics is again being considered in movement training for the actor. In addition to these theatre practitioners, the works of human movement specialists and body therapists, Feldenkrais, Alexander, and Laban have been included because they represent an important supplement to movement training in the post–World War II era. Much of the work of these three began out of a need to develop more healthful ways of living and working.

An increased need for knowledge of basic physiology, anatomy, and kinesics prompted a variety of new systems to spring forth. These not only included the works of Feldenkrais, Alexander, and Laban, but oriental theories such as t'ai chi, yoga, and t'ai kuan do, and Bioenergetics and Reiki as well. These latter systems exist from a point of view expressed by Barbara Weber Ray, founder of the American International Reiki Association.

> Life is made of energy, and energy is in perpetual motion, moving in swirling spirals. Each moment in your life is a new part of the unfolding spiral of your own life's process. The very essence of life is motion — nothing is status quo. Movement and change are basic, natural laws of energy — of life.[4]

Much of the focus in recent years has been directed toward these "body therapy" and Bioenergetic concepts in movement training in addition to the more traditional approaches suggested by Stanislavski, Grotowski, and Meyerhold.

We live in an age which offers dynamic and diversified approaches towards the training of the actor. Not only can we learn how to free our creative abilities through the sensory exercises of Stanislavski but we can reattach ourselves to the ritualistic nature of acting through the psychoanalytic language of gesture and "trance" theory of Grotowski. Additionally, we now approach a deeper understanding and appreciation of body development, physical exercise, energy control and focus, and proper alignment, balance, and posture through the works of Feldenkrais, Alexander, Laban and others who have enlightened us on the gestalt of the living, human artist.

Acting involves a person expressing truthful and honest attitudes and emotions in front of others in a theatrical presentation. These attitudes and emotions must be expressed by an actor who is comfortable in his presentation so as not to constrict his emotions or his vocal or physical performances. However realistic or symbolic his style may be, he must be concerned with how and why he speaks, moves, or thinks. This implies that a conscious decision must be made as to what and how he moves, and as in the case of improvisation, what he says. "Such work demands physical and vocal skill or craft, emotional stability, alert thinking, freedom of behavior, and confidence and trust in one's self and one's fellow actors."[5]

It is necessary to review briefly the major theories presented in this work in order to understand how they may be used in achieving the desired result of acting truthfully, honestly, and comfortably with respect to stage movement.

Most theatre historians prior to the twentieth century characterized Greek acting as a statue come to life—one which moved slowly and elegantly. Gestures and movements are described as being appropriate and fitting to the conventions of the theatre.[6] Movements were suggestive rather than realistic and predominately presentational. However, twentieth century historians have shed new light on the Greek theatre and the style of acting. James Allen suggested:

> Let us remind ourselves, further, that the ancient Greeks were a people whose emotions were easily stirred, and that with them, as among Greeks today, gesticulation was both free and expressive. It follows almost necessarily that their acting was characterized by easy and natural gestures, and that even emotional acting had a place, probably a large place, in their theatre. Indeed, it was an ancient Greek critic who wrote: "Whatever is unemotional is essentially undramatic"; and the plays abound in situations that demand an emotional expression.[7]

Michael Walton concurs in *The Greek Sense of Tragedy:* "the visual aspect of the Greek theatre has for so long taken second place to the spoken word . . . it is still the common belief that what was *said* in the Greek tragedies was more important than what was *seen.* It was not so."[8]

The modern actor who approaches a classical role must keep in mind that this style of theatre requires the highest level of physical control in addition to balance, flexibility, coordination, and poise.

Though the movements may be described as stylized by today's standards, certainly, they were expressive in nature. The modern actor involved in a study of the Greek style is introduced to a stylized, dance-like movement sense in which movements can be abstracted and internal emotions exhibited. This is a highly specialized manner of moving, one which requires much training. Actors, in the Greek sense of tragedy, do not move their characterizations, they dance them.

Martha Graham has done extensive work in her modern dances in the *abstract* style. We often hear the words abstract or abstraction in relation to modern dance, modern art, or modern theatre. The meaning of the word goes beyond avant-garde or modern. It actually is a bare-bones expression — an essence of expression. Another way of illustrating the term abstract is with the word *extract*. Consider that you were buying vanilla extract in a grocery store. The product in the bottle is the pure essence of vanilla — nothing more and nothing less. No additional ingredients have been included to mask the taste and aroma of vanilla. In abstract art or dance or theatre the same is true. Nonessential elements have been taken away so that what is left (or expressed) is the pure essence of an idea or emotion. We may look at dramatic abstraction as unrealistic because we do not recognize them in everyday life, yet the abstraction is the simplified extraction of our emotions and motivations. The Greeks knew this and used it in their theatre performances.

"Both drama and acting in ancient Rome were based largely on Greek models."[9] At first the Romans did not borrow the use of the mask, but later it was added. Much of Roman acting must have resembled Greek acting, the noted exception being in their style of movement.

> [T]he Romans, with their native mime talent, gave wide range to the development of acting, but placed emphasis on showmanship and virtuosity. The lavish praises given by Lucien to the art of pantomime, as well as the detailed instructions on the use of the hands given by Quintilian, are evidence of the refined, perhaps over-refined, delight in the external nuance of performance.[10]

This lively and physical approach to performance served as a predecessor to the commedia dell'arte style of theatre. It was also during the Roman period that the emotional identification of an actor with his character is first hinted.

Quintilian offered suggestions to the orator from the art of acting.

> His first principle . . . [is] "the prime essential for stirring the emotions
> of others is, in my opinion, first to feel those emotions oneself." This
> hand-me-down had already been worn threadbare by Aristotle, Horace,
> and Cicero. Yet Quintilian's complicating premise . . . casts the ques-
> tion in a different and far more interesting light.[11]

Quintilian's comment echoes Aristotle's like concern and he hints at
what Diderot and others continued to question. Quintilian's point of
view was that art (whether acting or oratory) should express attitudes
quite different from those same attitudes expressed in life. He offered
no definitive answers as to how this could be achieved.

The primary concerns of the actor involved in Roman drama,
especially Roman comedy and the commedia dell'arte style, are the
energetic, athletic, quick, and often acrobatic style of movements required for such roles. An understanding of this style may be developed
through a study of sports activities using Biomechanical techniques,
through stage combat devices, and through a study of pantomime
which develops clear and precise movements. While there is usually
little physical contact between characters in the Greek style, in the
Roman style there is considerable physical contact. Movements must be
able to be executed rapidly, forcefully, and with a high degree of
presentational skill.

The modern actor may have to adapt more severely for the Greek,
Roman, or commedia style than the sixteenth century or Elizabethan
style. Though professional acting was first established during the sixteenth century, the greatest emphasis in acting was placed on the voice
rather than the movements. Attention was given to more natural and
realistic gestures and movements during this time, yet by today's standards, the bodily actions were somewhat heightened and conventionalized. Gestures were not stereotyped; rather, actions were suited to
character, action, and emotion.

> Piecing together the brief references in plays and in anecdotes, we may
> say that the Elizabethan actor was distinguished primarily by his ex-
> cellent voice. He was expected to base his actions and gestures on the
> words of the poet and to act with decorum and modesty. . . .[12]

Much has been written on acting Shakespeare yet the greatest proportion of such writing is directed towards the text, the poetry or music of the lines, and the expressive use of voice. The movement training of the contemporary actor with respect to Shakespearean or Elizabethan drama should include exercises which develop coordination, strength, balance, grace and elegance, and ease of movement. Knowledge of period dance sequences is also often required. Although some natural and realistic movements are used, they are set against a posture and movement style which is characterized by a slightly elevated carriage, fluid motions, and presentationalism.

A comparison of movement styles between the Neoclassic and the Elizabethan periods reveals that the former is less realistic or natural. Neoclassicism borrowed heavily from the commedia style, hence the movements were presentational, theatrical, and highly stylized. This was especially true of the comedies. Movements were accented by their rapid execution and gestures were often used to punctuate spoken lines. When acting in this style actors must pay close attention to postural attitudes, long sequences of movement such as crosses, the use of small hand props and the influence of period costume on the movements.

The seventeenth century was characterized by a rhetorical style of acting. It was during this time that rigid rules of behavior and decorum were established. Movements were elevated to exaggerated poses and there was extensive use of curtsies, bows, and asides.

The eighteenth century brought on many of the most significant and drastic changes in acting to date. Innovations in science and technology were altering humans' views of themselves, their world, and their control of both. A new, so-called scientific study of phenomena emerged. Probing questions concerning the phenomenology of acting and theatre art were raised, primarily by Diderot.

Diderot represented an anti-emotionalist's point of view in acting. He suggested in his treatise on acting, *The Paradox of Acting,* that the actor approach his work as craft, something which could be learned, perfected, and performed. Diderot believed that the actor should possess a degree of objectivity. Further, "He must have in himself an unmoved and disinterested onlooker."[13] Through this method, according to Diderot, the actor was free to study his performance and calculate his actions. This gave acting consistency. "What confirms me in this view is the unequal acting of players who play from the heart. From them you must expect no unity. . . . Tomorrow they will miss the point they have excelled in today."[14]

Diderot was no doubt influenced by the most famous actor of the day, David Garrick. Garrick was considered to be a realistic actor, often using movements and gestures based on real life observances. He was a master of the study of acting and he proved to be versatile and ingenious. He acted, managed, and wrote plays, but most of all he should be remembered for embodying an age in which science and an attempt to understand the world were used to define art.

This interest in the scientific approach to acting was pervasive in the eighteenth and nineteenth centuries. Attempts were made over and over to codify and calculate the art of acting. No more strident attempts were made than through the works of François Delsarte.

Considerable energies were spent during this time in developing systems through which the actor could control his abilities. Delsarte's system was an attempt to codify gestures and movements in order to project emotions and character attitudes. This seems a natural extension of the earlier theories of Diderot and the acting style of David Garrick.

What these theories lend to the modern-day actor is an external approach to acting — a so-called "outside in" approach rather than an emotionally stimulated approach. This suggests that the modern actor should train his or her body so that it is adequately prepared to communicate a number of levels of experience and in such a way that those expressions can be rehearsed for exact re-presentation. Today Delsarte's system is an object of ridicule and scorn by those who demand emotional connection with external movements. Garrick's anti-emotionalism is also rejected. Yet they provided a springboard for new directions in actor training and stage movement. Aspects of Diderot's paradox are still considered today. Actors today experiment with the degree to which they are connected with their roles.

Much of our current attitudes concerning acting and stage movement are perceived through the influence of the twentieth century genius Constantin Stanislavski. Stanislavski was representative of an age of great change, also described as an age of realism. Life was revealed through a nonselective, nonromantic, "slice of life" manner. Rationalism and positivism were the key explanations of the day. In acting and playwriting truth, believability, and care of life-like detail were demanded.

Garrick and Delsarte sought to control the actor's expressiveness through objective, intellectual control. Stanislavski sought to inspire the actor through creative, emotional control. He refined his principles of acting to include emotional as well as physical exercises which would provide the actor with an unlimited source of creativity, inspiration, and imagination, all the while stressing the importance of being able to reproduce those aspects during repeated performances.

> Stanislavski believed, first of all, that the actor must experience real emotion, that he must identify with the character he is portraying, that he may use his own past emotional experiences, and above all, that he must learn to speak and behave naturally, as a human being in life.[15]

While Stanislavski's belief in the "felt emotions" of acting seems to contradict Diderot's lack of feeling, the two do agree about the actor's control of his acting. This could be accomplished through the method of physical actions outlined by Stanislavski. Our modern attitudes toward stage movement and movement training for the actor are centered, though not always directly, on this method of physical actions. Sonia Moore, author of *The Stanislavski Method,* explains how the method of physical actions enables the actor to control his inspiration and emotion.

> Since the psychological and the physical in the human being are indivisibly united, truthful fulfillment of the physical action involves an actor's truthful emotions. The physical action is the "bait" for an emotion. It is, however, important to understand that Stanislavski also considered the spoken word a physical action. All of Stanislavski's searching was directed toward finding control over the moments of inspiration, and he developed favorable conditions for such control. Inspiration is the result of conscious work by an actor who has mastered the technique.[16]

The modern actor may employ the method of physical actions as a means of expressing emotion and state of being. Stanislavski suggested dance training for actors to increase their physical dexterity. This would be helpful to the modern actor in addition to much of the body therapy work which frees the body and strengthens it. Feldenkrais and Alexander's body awareness techniques are highly recommended since they can accomplish the extreme sensitivity of mind and body of which Stanislavski wrote so often.

Long overshadowed by his contemporaries, Vsevolod Meyerhold's contributions in the area of movement focus on his system of Biomechanics. Hoover states:

> Biomechanics or the Biomechanical System of Vs. Meyerhold attempts to establish laws of movement for actors in stage space; by experimentation it devises set exercises for training and works out methods of the actor's art based on exact calculation and regulation of the actor's conduct on stage.[17]

The greatest gift that Meyerhold offers to the modern actor is in the training program which he outlined some sixty years ago. His workshop program fits into what is called for today by many movement practitioners: the study of anatomy and physiology, dance training, rhythmic gymnastics, pantomime, and a study of how the voice and body interrelate. The modern student of acting can easily incorporate many aspects of Biomechanics into a comprehensive stage movement study. Such aspects as the correction of physical and vocal defects and the control of energy focus through physical means correspond directly to much of the work presented by Feldenkrais, Alexander, Lowen's Bioenergetics and other contemporary movement theories.

From the pre–World War II influences we have moved to the eclectic style of the postwar era. Spearheaded by the doctrine of Antonin Artaud and embodied by the 1960s and 1970s work of Jerzy Grotowski and his Polish Laboratory Theatre, the theatre once again approached its ancient ritualistic heritage. Grotowski reduced and refined the art of acting back to its original roots — to the essential actor. The training of the actor's body was essential for Grotowski. He believed the mind and body of the actor must be reborn in the character. The total educational training of the actor could be achieved only through rigorous, strenuous, and disciplined effort. Grotowski referred to his study of the actor's art as "a parascientific research in the field."[18] He, too, searched for a scientific understanding of the phenomenological experience of acting.

From Diderot to Delsarte, from Stanislavski and Meyerhold to Grotowski and modern acting practitioners, the study and analysis of how the actor involves himself in the character are attempted to pursue a provable, observable, and scientific direction.

The latter decades of the twentieth century have brought us to a deeper and more mature understanding of the expressive forces of the human organism. The questions remain the same. It is our approach to the solutions which has changed. In a constant effort to understand how to act we have altered the way we act.

Today, the contemporary actor may align himself with the Stanislavski method, or he may pursue study in the more experimental, "poor" theatre concept of Grotowski. Further, the actor may approach the training program of Biomechanics. Any or all of these may include additional training or experimentation with Feldenkrais, Alexander, Laban, Oriental techniques, dance training, or Bioenergetics. The modern theatre is truly eclectic and the actor's movement training must be also.

> The contemporary actor should be familiar with and capable of using techniques ranging from Stanislavski to Brecht to Artaud to Grotowski to Chaikin to Bob Fosse to Michael Bennett to Tommy Tune to Hal Prince. The actor should understand human emotion and know when and how to use it or restrict it. . . .
>
> The contemporary theatre offers a continually expanding experience for actors. The demands imposed upon the actor are astonishing. He should not only study his role . . . but also relate his own psychical and physical beings to those of a character.[19]

The contemporary actor should not strive so much towards a separate understanding of these theorists in their application of stage movement but rather towards what each has in common. Though they are often interpreted as having opposing views, quite often a comparative study reveals they are, in actuality, saying the same thing only with different words.

What we need in movement training for the actor is a general philosophy which encompasses a definition of movement for the actor, movement training techniques, and certification or standardization for movement trainers or specialists.

Some administrators may say that they would be happy to have a movement person but that their budgets do not allow for "specialists." I
believe that this attitude represents the "expendability" of this skill,
along with those of voice and speech. During our lifetimes western
theatre has been performed primarily from the neck up, and in too
many theatre departments this now historical phenomenon still
prevails. Despite the trendy notion of an integrated approach to acting-
voice-movement there is a real lack of interest on the part of chairs to
hire in movement, voice, or speech. I have heard a number of laments
regarding student actor's inability to move or speak properly, but there
is a general reluctance by any but the largest departments to hire someone to deal specifically with these skills. If actors can get acting classes
and learn to "feel" then chairs believe the needs of the students are being
met. The average non-theatre person is full of feelings, and many express these feelings quite well in their daily lives, but that does not make
them actors. No other performing art pays so little attention to technical
skills as does the theatre. Musicians, singers, and dancers take technique
classes their entire performing lives.[20]

Actors and actor trainers face many artistic, economic, and
philosophical questions today. In addition to preparing themselves for
their craft and cultivating their talents they must focus on the type of
training they wish to receive. Whether studying privately, in regional
or professional theatre groups, or in a university or college program, actors will no doubt be exposed to a wide variety of movement and voice
training in addition to a variety of acting styles and techniques.

At the 1988 convention of the Association for Theatre in Higher
Education (ATHE) the task force on standards for training the theatre
movement specialist began to clarify some of the assumptions and con-
fusions which surround present-day movement training precepts. They
began with the terminology itself.

Movement for actors includes basic body training, anatomy and
physiology, training techniques such as Feldenkrais and Alexander, and
movement theories like those of Lowen, Laban, Alexander, Pisk, and
others. *Theatre movement* refers to specific performance skills such as
period dance, combat skills, and dance training. *Stage movement* encompasses all movement on the stage which includes blocking and stage
business. More specifically, stage movement includes posture, gestures,
mannerisms, and bodily movements. In fact, stage movement comprises the total visual effect of the actor on the stage.

But the visual representation does not only offer itself for the spectator, for indeed, the outer manifestation of "character" is connected to the inner workings of the actor, his emotions, motivations, and understanding of the character. Throughout the history of acting the relationship between mind-body and character portrayal has been the focal point of the craft of acting. The need for movement training seems evident. If training in this area is not included we limit the aesthetic and creative growth of the actor and, ultimately, the theatre which he inhabits. If we accept that movement training is needed to some degree at some level of the actor's training then we must answer a number of questions.

1. Who should be responsible for the stage movement training of the actor?

2. What sort of facilities are needed in order to train the actor and his body properly?

3. What type of movement training should be included in a basic acting program? What type of movement training should be included for the professional actor, the actor who needs advanced work, or the actor with specialized needs such as acting in historical plays, plays with dance or movement sequences, or extreme physical demands for a role?

These questions are not answered easily, but in theatre settings throughout the world similar questions are addressed on a daily basis. According to Lynn Norris most "make do."[21] Ideally, a movement specialist should be responsible for the training of the actor and his body. Here we face still other questions.

4. If a movement specialist is responsible for such training how do we train a movement specialist?

5. What movement theories or movement experience should be included in a movement trainers program?

6. How do we certify such teachers?

Help in finding answers to these questions is provided by findings presented by a number of professional organizations and by the trial and error method of professionals who have experienced the problem of how to train the actor.

The answer to the question of who should be responsible for movement training is "a qualified movement specialist." A movement specialist is one who has studied stage movement specifically as it pertains to the stage actor. This is quite apart from dance training, mime, or stage combat, though a stage movement specialist should have experience in these areas along with other skills. A movement specialist must be able to recognize organic body problems and suggest alternatives to traditional exercise programs. First and foremost a movement specialist, through experience as a body therapist, dance teacher, specialist in Feldenkrais, Alexander, yoga or physiology and anatomy, must be able to assist any actor in his struggles to overcome the physical or psychophysical obstacles which often arise during rehearsal or training.

The movement specialist's task is, it seems, to spot problems before they occur, for often actors are not consciously aware of organic or physical problems. Primary in all physical work for the actor is to become more flexible, strong, and coordinated in all physical movements. This is a prerequisite to any further study of acting. Lynn Norris, a movement specialist, recalls the difficulties of dealing with a wide variety of student actors.

> Those students who are the most difficult, i.e. extreme over- or under-weight, severe psycho-physical manifestations, medical problems like hernias, epilepsy, brain damage, removed organs, spinal malfunctions (I have dealt with all of these), are left to perish because you cannot spend the time they need. The ones who will survive on their own, the high school athlete and the young women who have been dancing since they were three, will somehow get by on their own. Those in the middle who have posture problems, unconscious physical mannerisms, or mild psychophysical problems will fall to your lot, and if you do not whip them into shape in one year your methods will be challenged.... The fact that your charges are still growing physically and are wrestling with problems that have physical manifestations — i.e. drugs, alcohol, sex, little sleep, dorm food — and that you may have few amenities with which to work do not matter.[22]

Movement specialists face a formidable task considering that they are in charge of a variety of actors who themselves come from a variety of experience and backgrounds and have individual needs. These specialists must be able to spot physical problems, order some type of therapeutic system to reduce the problem, and also offer creative exercises which will direct actors in their efforts to shape their role.

The work of the specialist and the actor must occur in a proper environment. If specific instruction is offered in movement, certain considerations must be given to a movement space. Ideally the space should have a wooden floor or some such material which does not cause damage to knee, ankle, and hip joints during vigorous workouts. Often much of the physical work is conducted on the floor. Feldenkrais and Alexander technique alike request that the student lie on the floor, roll from a prone to sitting position, and at times, kneel. Other movement explorations require students to lie flat, then roll both legs over the head to extend and relax the lower back. Such movements place extreme pressure on the neck and shoulders if not done on a proper flooring.

The space should also include mirrors in order for students to observe their own progress. Most dance classes are conducted with the aid of mirrors so that dancers can observe movements and the body structure during movement. This tool is often helpful for actors working on posture, gesture, or integrated body structure. Controllable lighting, musical or rhythmic instruments, individual mats, and access to video taping equipment and films are of additional benefit for the actor in movement training. The use of dance or exercise studios may provide much of the needed space for actors and stage movement specialists.

Many theatre and university departments employ a movement trainer on staff and a room or space may be used for such training. This fulfills only part of the need. The training program itself must be comprehensive and intensive if actors are to be readied for the work ahead. Such a program should take a minimum of three years to complete.

> We have not been able to impress chairs with the necessity of a minimum of three years movement training for undergraduate acting majors. We have not helped administrators to see that many vocal and speech problems can be solved by adequate body work. We have not convinced them that it takes a year to get most students comfortable with moving before one can develop character work, period studies, combat, dance for nondancers, and creative movement on a sound basic structure. The idea of a BFA or MFA program without movement every semester perpetuates a lie.[23]

Historically, much of the student actor's work has been involved in text analysis, character analysis, acting style, and speech and diction study. All of these are important in the actor's training, but without movement and body work, actors will not be able to produce a characterization, and they will be limited in the types of roles they may be chosen for in the future. Movement and body work require intensive study for the changes do not occur quickly. Students must be made aware of the changes which need to be made; they must become sensitive to their bodies and the nuances which can be communicated by subtle movements, and they must often involve themselves in a retraining program to rid themselves of old habits and physical clichés.

Acting teachers can provide help to student actors in the preliminaries of body work such as relaxation, flexibility, coordination, balance, and strength. But where are the acting teachers (without specialized movement training) who can deal with the severe organic physical problems of some actors, the psychophysical concern of extreme stage fright or anxiety, in addition to the occasional need of stage combat, mime, acrobatic skills, or historical, social, ethnic, and tap dance sequences?

Many actors have had extensive experience on the stage through children's theatre programs, community theatre work, and secondary school productions. Upon entering advanced study in college, professional school, resident theatre, or private training, they are confronted with an intensive curriculum focusing primarily on the craft of acting. Many student actors in this situation are at "square one" despite the amount of experience they may have had in performing. In addition, many students may have had an interest in acting prior to college but do not have experience.

During the first two years of study (whether for the student actor with experience or the novice that now declares an acting major) certain fundamentals of stage movement must be established. These fundamentals include basic relaxation techniques, motor skills that increase flexibility, strength, endurance, coordination, balance, and flow or grace, a survey of movement analysis theories, dance for the non-dancer (this includes historical styles, tap, social, and period dance for the actor), corrective skills, and specialized movement skills such as stage combat, tumbling/gymnastics, and mime. Actors must be impressed with the fact that they, like dancers and athletes, must approach their body work with the attitude that it is a lifelong, cumulative process, not something which once acquired can be left unattended.

Once we begin to accept that stage movement must be included in an actor's total range of study and with considerable time and effort spent specifically on the study of movement, we are led to the concerns of how to train the movement specialist. A specialized study of movement for the actor has come into its own over the last two decades partly because of the influence of such techniques as Feldenkrais and Alexander, and, especially, because a need was voiced by acting practitioners. The need is clear yet the solution elusive. Lynn Norris suggests that

> Our own lack of a definition for the basis of sound actor training, our very disparate backgrounds, and the dearth of structured teacher training programs for those who will teach actors have left us, as movement teachers, with a shifting ground on which to stand and center.[24]

Some movement trainers have specialized study in Stanislavski's systems. Others have experience in Alexander, Feldenkrais, Linklater, or Lessac and still others come from a background of yoga, t'ai chi and Eastern movement systems. A large number of specialists have crossed over from dance backgrounds which include classical ballet, modern dance techniques, and other dance techniques. Others have exercise science and kinesiological backgrounds. These various fields of study represent a formidable number of practitioners who have, for one reason or another, left their primary field and have chosen to work with actors, thus utilizing their unique experiences all in an effort to compose a comprehensive method of training. To expect these members with their separate backgrounds to have a single approach to movement training for the actor is impossible. However, a movement specialist should be familiar with the techniques represented by the preceding in addition to secondary skills and an in-depth knowledge of acting and the theatre.

We live in an age of specialization and specialists. Individuals are often sent to "a specialist" throughout their daily lives, whether it be a physician, a plumber, or a teacher. Jennifer Martin, a movement specialist with the former American Theatre Association, responded to a panel discussion on theatre movement with the following:

It was generally agreed that basic work must precede specialized skills, but a quick survey clearly showed a wide divergence of approach. A few use one basic movement system such as Feldenkrais or Alexander, but most would characterize their approach as eclectic, combining and adapting from many sources those movement experiences which best suit their student's needs. There was an additional approach which, in a sense, combined the basic work with learning specific skills. . . .

The consensus, then, was that with the exception of anatomy, kinesiology, and correctives, which are absolutely essential for any stage movement teachers regardless of approach, no particular body of information and experience should be considered mandatory. Rather, the focus should be on the student's development of his own self-awareness. [25]

The purpose of theatre movement for the movement specialist is to open and free the student actor to be able to take charge of his role. This goes beyond teaching a set of skills or imposing a specific technique on the actor. The role of the theatre movement specialist is to act as guide for the actor, a guide who knows the territory and can troubleshoot any problems which may present themselves. And if problems arise, it is the movement trainer who can devise, out of his or her wide base of knowledge and experience, a plan of action to aid the actor in overcoming those obstacles. For example, a movement specialist with specific training in stage combat may utilize some Feldenkrais exercises in encouraging flexibility and strength while at the same time teaching specific combat moves. Another specialist trained in Laban's Effort/Shape may utilize Stanislavski's method of physical actions to rehearse a specific scene while at the same time encouraging the student to become aware of the flow, energy, or weight resistance of the actions of stage business. Work in Alexander technique may be used to relax the body while strengthening the voice of an actor who is working on a character requiring extreme physical demands, such as the Elephant Man, or Shakespeare performed in an athletic, commedia style.

The combinations of different movement training techniques are virtually limitless but may prove useless unless the trainer is familiar with a number of techniques. Ideally, movement specialists must have a working knowledge of the role stage movement has played in acting throughout the history of acting. Otherwise they would be stepping "cold" into a situation where their expertise was needed.

As already presented in this study, the attitudes toward movement have changed vastly from the Greeks to Stanislavski and in the contemporary theatre. In any program in which the theatre movement specialist works, the season may include a Greek tragedy, a Shakespearean comedy, a production of Ibsen's theatre of realism, and an avant-garde, absurdist drama. The needs of such a season are vast, varied, and complex. But what if the production staff or faculty is limited to four or even two persons, as is the case in many community theaters or educational theatres? The panel studying such problems at the American Theatre Association in 1978 made some suggestions,

> First, designate one of those faculty members as movement coach and begin to provide the necessary training to help him/her fill areas of deficiencies. That process may begin by taking anatomy and kinesiology courses, then using summers, sabbaticals, and school vacations to take workshops or intensive programs with recognized leaders in stage movement training.[26]

Through continued study many of today's acting teachers could become movement specialists as well, thus assuring movement as a part of an integrated study program for actors.

The question of certification for movement specialists exists in the minds of those who want additional insurance that their movement trainer be someone who has demonstrated a mastery of certain fundamental training principles. Why could movement specialists be certified when teachers of acting and directing are not certified? The answer is they do not have to be certified. Their reputation, like that of teachers of acting, directing, design or playwriting, rests in their work and in the comments shared by past students and followers.

But a movement specialist is a representative of a specific area of study, one which is closely aligned with one's body, health, and at times, state of mind. Oftentimes we require proof of one's training and expertise when dealing with our bodies and our health. Physical therapists, physicians, psychological counselors and other health-related practitioners require state or board certification. This is not to suggest that movement specialists be certified by the state, but it is to suggest that it be done by a governing board which has established certain minimum criteria for study in the chosen field. Dance therapists have much of the same certification requirements and these are maintained by professional organizations.

The Theatre Movement Program of the University/College Theatre Association under the head of the American Theatre Association would have been the logical body to oversee such certification, and in fact it did attempt such a program. But with the demise of the ATA in 1986 the responsibility fell to other professional organizations such as the American Educational Theatre Association and the American Theatre in Higher Education. Both associations are relatively new and have reorganized. Certification standards and criteria for movement specialists are a concern. The Task Force on Training the Theatre Movement Specialist submitted minimum criteria in August 1988; a movement specialist should have:

1. Training and experience in acting and/or directing.

2. Knowledge of body sciences including anatomy and physiology, kinesiology, and motor learning.

3. Knowledge in one or more of the self-awareness programs such as Alexander, Feldenkrais, and Aston Patterning.

4. Knowledge of and extended training in at least one movement theory including Delsarte, Laban, Pisk, Alexander, Feldenkrais, Lowen.

5. Knowledge of physical characterization techniques including effort-shape work, neutral and character mask work, semantics, and so on.

6. Knowledge of one or more performance skills such as combat, mime, dance, or period dance; and

7. Some knowledge of related disciplines such as aerobics, martial arts or gymnastics.

Great strides have been made in the last two decades towards an improved attitude in movement training for the actor. However, the current listing of movement as a separate and specialized aspect of actor training testifies that much lies ahead. If we can agree and accept that a minimum standard must be established concerning the environment in which movement is taught, the principles of movement which are taught, and the minimum standards by which movement instructors are trained, then much of our future work will prove easier and, ultimately, more beneficial for the acting students.

Those who direct acting programs and those who teach acting (and especially movement for the actor) must commit themselves to a new approach to actor training. Roger Gross states this call as follows:

> So, we must not turn away from the promise of the new actor training, and the risks come with the territory. The challenge has been put to this generation of acting teachers. Now we will see what we are made of. The burden of self-re-education will be tremendous in time, effort, and money. My time with Alexander Lowen, the top man in bioenergetics, cost me $60 an hour. My Alexander Technique work was moderate: only $25 an hour. T'ai Chi Ch'uan was a bargain at $20 an hour. All are essential, and this is just a beginning. There are anatomy, physiology, kinesiology, first aid, CPR, speech science, neurobiology, kinesics, proxemics, semantics, etcetera, etcetera. Repeat: all essential. Essential because, as acting teachers, we presume to tinker with people's bodies and minds at a profound level. This is not business for dilettantes.[27]

Ultimately, the actor teaches himself. Through a trial and error method he experiments and tests what works and what does not produce positive results. But quite often the inexperienced actor and, at times, the accomplished actor face similar problems. It is then up to the trainer, teacher, specialist, or coach to offer solutions to the specific problems faced by the actor. This is where the movement specialist is vital. Not necessarily as one who possesses all of the answers, or even as one who is experienced in all techniques, methods, therapies, or systems, but as guide and resource person.

The movement trainer should be able to instill in the actor a comprehensive, wide spectrum of abilities and methods so that the actor can best approach a role outside of the context of his training. Jack Clay states, "What the actor needs is a unified self-use training based on a study of the fundamentals of his body mechanics and his energy systems."[28] The self-use training may come from a variety of sources which the actor deems beneficial. It is the role of the movement trainer to provide the initial introduction to a variety of means.

> The development of self-use training for the performer seems to me one of the most important activities in actor training today. . . . Our older acting training was too narrowly focused on acting as thinking. The new emphasis shares with the newer psychologies the breakdown of the old body-vs.-mind dichotomy.[29]

In today's movement training for the actor we need not discard the old training methods but rather add to the existing knowledge. We are only now able to judge objectively the outcome of the Stanislavski–Strasberg Actor's Studio method of acting. The influence of Grotowski, though pervasive, has still not found its way into the majority of acting programs. One can only speculate at the outcome of a generation of actors with a full and comprehensive movement training program as part of their overall study.

All programs which attempt to train actors should include studies in the aesthetics of theatre, acting styles and methods, considerable vocal study which encompasses vocal production, diction, accents, and vocal development for the stage; text analysis, theatre history, and studies which prepare the actor for the business of acting. These include makeup styles and application, audition techniques, and television and film acting techniques. This latter, of course, would add years of additional work for the actor in training. Much of the basis of the art is the same whether for audience or cameras.

The foregoing are a prerequisite for any attempt at advanced training. Time, effort, and study in movement for the actor should be extensive. If included in a college program, three years or six semesters of work should be directed in stage movement. This is in addition to traditional acting classes, play or text analysis classes, or voice and diction instruction.

These six semesters should include a combination of the following courses. Sequences may vary according to the thrust of the acting program, i.e. musical theatre emphasis, Elizabethan and classic orientation, teacher education theatre majors, or preprofessional acting majors.

• Introduction to movement principles—an investigation and study of the basic principles of movement. Proxemics, kinesics, physiology and anatomical fundamentals as they apply to stage movement and the actor working on a role.

• Survey of movement analysis theories—a psychological and psychophysical approach to the study of how movement reveals personality, emotion, and state of being. Laban's Effort/Shape theory, Stanislavski's method of physical actions, and background information on the scientific and psychologically based approach to movement analysis included.

- Survey of historical movement styles—a history of acting through a study of period movement, gesture, mannerisms, and posture through a study of the music, painting, and plays of the period as outlined by Stanislavski.

- Diagnostic and corrective skills—an introduction to body awareness and the beneficial or negative manners in which our carriage, posture, and movement patterns affect our overall creative and artistic expressions. Primary work would be conducted in the Feldenkrais and Alexander techniques, though some avant-garde programs might include Bioenergetics, Reiki, neurolinguistic studies, or any of a number of recent theories. Relaxation skills stressed. These include yoga, meditation, t'ai chi and exercises on relaxation and concentration proposed by Stanislavski, Grotowski, and Chaikin.

- Special movement skills—an introduction to stage combat, basic acrobatic and gymnastic skills, mime, and dance for the non-dancer. Stage combat may include Oriental or Western influences. An investigation of Meyerhold's Biomechanical exercises must be incorporated into the acrobatic and gymnastic work. Dance for the non-dancer could best serve the actor if a modern approach were used. Erick Hawkin's technique is based on relaxation. His dance and movement technique is expressed in anatomical terms which is of great benefit for the actor with limited dance training. Alwin Nikolais and Murray Louis both use improvisational work extensively in their training. These techniques offer great creative stimulus while also building strength, flexibility, and coordination.

Movement techniques for the actor should include anatomical work, technique work and relaxation work, as well as improvisational work.

In professional theatre jargon the actor of today must be a "triple threat"—singer, dancer, and actor. No longer will great acting skills or a powerful voice be enough to assure him or her of consistent employment. The trainers and teachers of would-be professional actors must be equally trained in order to prepare their students for the harsh realities of a life in the theatre. Actors today are required to be more than actors—they must be performers, entertainers, artists, interpreters, vocalists, and especially, movers. Movement trainers who work with today's acting students must meet this new challenge. Acting programs must accept the need of a comprehensive movement training curriculum. The main objective of such a program is the integration of mind and body and the various systems available which can stimulate and control that relationship.

The most advantageous movement training program for today's actors is one which recognizes and values work done in the past. It also incorporates more recent theories and systems, especially those which work in harmony. This is accomplished through a blending of each of the major theories discussed in this study. What Feldenkrais and Alexander have to say about proper alignment and relaxation complements Stanislavski's belief in concentration and energy. Laban's Effort/Shape blends well with Meyerhold's value of spatial relationships and the efficiency of movement. Grotowski in many ways required all of these for his theatre—abstraction, concentration, energy focus, and movement as the essential expression.

What we must do now is to take what each theorist has laid before us and use it to create a more artistic theatre experience. We, as actors, directors, and movement specialists must meet the challenge of modern theatre—to project characters artistically and believably, to express character as a thinking, feeling, and moving entity, and to express character in the boldest manifestation or the most subtle nuance through voice and body.

Chapter Notes

Introduction

1. Joseph R. Roach, *The Player's Passion* (Newark: University of Delaware Press, 1985), p. 11.
2. *Ibid.*, pp. 12–13.
3. Jean Sabatine, *The Actor's Image: Movement Training for Stage and Screen,* collaborator, David Hodges (Englewood Cliffs, N.J.: Prentice-Hall, 1983), p. 4.
4. Valentina Litvinoff, "The Natural and the Stylized: In Conflict or Harmony?" printed in *Movement for the Actor,* ed. Lucille S. Rubin (New York: Drama Books Specialists, 1980), p. 104.
5. Patsy Ann Clark Hecht, "Kinetic Techniques for the Actor: An Analysis and Comparison of the Movement Training Systems of François Delsarte, Emile Jaques-Dalcroze, and Rudolf Laban" (Ph.D. dissertation, Wayne State University, Detroit, 1971), pp. 3–4.

1. The Legacy of the Sacred Circle

1. Benjamin Hunningher, *The Origin of Theatre* (Westport, Conn.: Greenwood Press, 1978), p. 13.
2. *Ibid.*, pp. 16–17.
3. David Cole, *The Theatrical Event: A Mythos, a Vocabulary, a Perspective* (Middleton, Conn.: Wesleyan University Press, 1975), pp. 7–8.
4. Oscar G. Brockett, *History of the Theatre* (Boston: Allyn and Bacon, 1982), p. 6.
5. Joseph Campbell, *The Hero with a Thousand Faces* (Princeton, N.J.: Princeton University Press, 1972), p. 3.

2. The Greeks: A Theatre of Spectacle

1. Aristotle, *On Man and the Universe: Poetics,* trans. by Samuel Henry Butcher (Roslyn, N.Y.: Walter J. Black, Inc., 1943), p. 422.
2. *Ibid.*, pp. 426–427.

3. Marvin Carlson, *Theories of the Theatre: A Historical and Critical Survey, from the Greeks to the Present* (Ithaca, N.Y.: Cornell University Press, 1984), p. 17.

4. Margarete Bieber, *The History of the Greek and Roman Theatre* (Princeton, N.J.: Princeton University Press, 1961), p. 9.

5. *Ibid.*, pp. 27–28.

6. *Ibid.*, p. 82.

7. Michael Walton, *The Greek Sense of Tragedy* (New York: Methuen, 1984), p. 65.

8. Bieber, *The History of the Greek and Roman Theatre*, pp. 81–82.

9. Walton, *The Greek Sense of Tragedy*, p. 59.

10. *Ibid.*, p. 68.

11. Edwin Duerr, *The Length and Depth of Acting* (New York: Holt, Rinehart, 1962), p. 32.

12. Walton, *The Greek Sense of Theatre*, p. 3.

3. The Romans: Oratory and Entertainment

1. Roach, *The Player's Passion*, p. 24.

2. *Ibid.*, p. 27.

3. Lucian, "On Pantomime," reprinted in part in *Actors on Acting*, ed. Toby Cole and Helen Krich Chinoy (New York: Crown Publishers, 1970), pp. 32–33.

4. Bieber, *The History of the Greek and Roman Theatre*, p. 162.

5. Roach, *The Player's Passion*, p. 27.

4. The Sixteenth and Seventeenth Centuries: Elizabethan and Rhetorical

1. Roach, *The Player's Passion*, p. 29.

2. *Ibid.*, p. 30.

5. The Eighteenth Century: Garrick and Diderot

1. Roach, *The Player's Passion*, p. 56.

2. David Garrick, "An Essay on Acting," reprinted in *Actors on Acting*, ed. Toby Cole and Helen Krich Chinoy (New York: Crown Publishers, 1970), p. 134.

3. Roach, *The Player's Passion*, p. 59.

4. *Ibid.*

5. *Ibid.*, p. 95.

6. *Ibid.*, p. 117.

7. Denis Diderot, *The Paradox of Acting* (New York: Hill and Wang, 1957), p. 20.

8. Carlson, *Theories of the Theatre*, p. 153.

9. Roach, *The Player's Passion*, pp. 141–142.

10. *Ibid.*, p. 161.

6. Subjective Idealism: Romanticism and Delsarte

1. Patsy Ann Clark Hecht, "Kinetic Techniques for the Actor," p. 55.
2. François Delsarte, "Elements of the Delsarte System," reprinted in *Actors on Acting*, ed. by Toby Cole and Helen Krich Chinoy (New York: Crown Publishers, 1970), p. 187.
3. Carlson, *Theories of the Theatre*, p. 219.
4. Patsy Ann Clark Hecht, "Kinetic Techniques for the Actor," pp. 77–78.

7. The Early Twentieth Century: Constantin Stanislavski

1. Christine Edwards, *The Stanislavski Heritage* (New York: New York University Press, 1965), p. 35.
2. *Ibid.*, p. 43.
3. *Ibid.*, p. 58.
4. Roach, *The Player's Passion*, p. 206.
5. Sonia Moore, *Training an Actor: The Stanislavski System in Class* (New York: Penguin Books, 1980), p. 34.
6. Constantin Stanislavski, *Creating a Role* (New York: Theatre Arts Books, 1949), p. 62.
7. Roach, *The Player's Passion*, p. 218.

8. Meyerhold's Biomechanics

1. James Symons, *Meyerhold's Theatre of the Grotesque* (Coral Gables, Fla.: University of Miami Press, 1971), p. 15.
2. Old style refers to the Julian calendar dates which are 12 days behind the Gregorian calendar.
3. In 1895 he changed his name to Vsevolod Emilevich Meyerhold, thus dropping the Jewish-sounding "g" to "h."
4. Symons, *Meyerhold's Theatre of the Grotesque*, p. 23.
5. *Ibid.*, p. 24.
6. Constantin Stanislavski, *My Life in Art*, trans. by J. J. Robbin (New York: Theatre Arts Books, 1957), p. 429.
7. Toby Cole and Helen Krich Chinoy, *Actors on Acting* (New York: Crown Publishers, 1970), p. 501.
8. Mel Gordon, "Meyerhold's Biomechanics," *Drama Review*, Spring, 1974, p. 73.
9. Vsevolod Meyerhold, *Meyerhold on Theatre*, trans. and ed. by Edward Braun (New York: Hill and Wang, 1969), p. 25.
10. Oscar Brockett, *History of the Theatre*, 4th ed. (Boston: Allyn and Bacon, 1982), p. 614.
11. C. Moody, "Meyerhold and the Commedia dell'Arte," *Modern Language Review*, October, 1978, p. 859.
12. Meyerhold, *Meyerhold on Theatre*, p. 147.
13. Gordon, "Meyerhold's Biomechanics," pp. 73–74.
14. *Ibid.*, p. 75.
15. *Ibid.*, p. 76.

16. Roach, *The Player's Passion*, p. 198.
17. *Ibid.*, pp. 198–199.
18. Gordon, "Meyerhold's Biomechanics," p. 77.
19. Marjorie Hoover, *Meyerhold: The Art of Conscious Theatre* (Amherst: University of Massachusetts Press, 1974), p. 100.
20. *Ibid.*
21. C. Moody, "Meyerhold and the Commedia dell'Arte," p. 869.
22. Meyerhold, *Meyerhold on Theatre*, p. 198.
23. *Ibid.*, p. 200.
24. John Martin, "How Meyerhold Trains His Actors," *Theatre Guild Magazine*, November, 1930, p. 26.
25. *Ibid.*
26. *Ibid.*, p. 28.
27. *Ibid.*, p. 20.
28. Hoover, *Meyerhold: The Art of Conscious Theatre*, p. 280.

9. Postmodern Trends: Jerzy Grotowski

1. C.W.E. Bigsby, *A Critical Introduction to Twentieth Century American Drama, Volume Three: Beyond Broadway* (Cambridge, England: Cambridge University Press, 1985), p. 59.
2. Jennifer Kumiega, *The Theatre of Grotowski* (New York: Methuen, 1985), p. xi.
3. Grotowski's phrase.
4. Jerzy Grotowski, *Towards a Poor Theatre* (New York: Simon and Schuster, 1968), p. 16.
5. Kumiega, *The Theatre of Grotowski*, p. 6.
6. *Ibid.*, pp. 7–8.
7. Jan Kott, "On Grotowski—A Series of Critiques," *The Drama Review*, Winter, 1970, p. 199.
8. Kumiega, *The Theatre of Grotowski*, p. 10.
9. *Ibid.*, p. 12.
10. *Ibid.*, p. 201.
11. *Ibid.*, p. 215.
12. "Pogadanka o teatrze dla mlodziezy szkolnej" [school programme broadcast by Polish radio, October, 1979], *Dialog* 1980 nr: pp. 132–137 in Kumiega, *The Theatre of Grotowski*, p. 235.
13. Carlson, *Theories of the Theatre*, p. 454.
14. Daniel E. Cushman, "Grotowski: His Twentieth Anniversary," *Theatre Journal*, December, 1979, p. 460.
15. Grotowski, *Towards a Poor Theatre*, pp. 20–21.
16. "Grotowski's Seminar," *Time*, November 28, 1969, p. 71.
17. *Ibid.*
18. Cushman, "Grotowski: His Twentieth Anniversary," p. 460.
19. Grotowski, *Towards a Poor Theatre*, p. 16.
20. *Ibid.*, p. 193.
21. Cushman, "Grotowski: His Twentieth Anniversary," pp. 461–463.
22. Philip Auslander, "Holy Theatre and Catharsis," *Theatre Research International*, Spring, 1984, p. 16.

23. Grotowski, *Towards a Poor Theatre*, p. 52.
24. *Ibid.*, p. 142.
25. Timothy J. Wiles, *The Theatre Event: Modern Theories of Performance* (Chicago: University of Chicago Press, 1980), p. 152.
26. Auslander, "Holy Theatre and Catharsis," p. 26.
27. *Ibid.*, p. 28.
28. Andreas Freund, "Performance from Poland," *New Republic*, July 30, 1966, p. 36.
29. Grotowski preferred the term "process" to "method."
30. Kumiega, *The Theatre of Grotowski*, p. 111.
31. E. Barba, "The Kathakali Theatre," *The Drama Review*, Summer, 1967, p. 38.
32. *Ibid.*, p. 52.
33. *Ibid.*, pp. 162–163.
34. Grotowski, *Towards a Poor Theatre*, pp. 255–256.
35. J. L. Styan, *Drama, Stage, and Audience* (New York: Cambridge University Press, 1975), p. 141.
36. *Ibid.*, p. 150.
37. Igor Ilinsky, "Biomechanics," reprinted in *Actors on Acting*, ed. by Toby Cole and Helen Krich Chinoy (New York: Crown Publishers, 1970), pp. 504–505.
38. Paul Schmidt, ed., *Meyerhold at Work* (Austin: University of Texas Press, 1980), p. xiv.
39. Jan Kott, "After Grotowski: The End of the Impossible Theatre," trans. Krystyna Bittenek, *Theatre Quarterly* 10 (Summer, 1980): p. 31.
40. Julian M. Olf, "Acting and Being: Some Thoughts about Metaphysics and Modern Performance Theory," *Theatre Journal* 33 (March, 1981): p. 42.
41. Richard Schechner, "An Interview with Grotowski," *Tulane Drama Review*, 13 (Fall 1968): p. 32.
42. Grigori V. Kristi, "The Training of an Actor in the Stanislavski School of Acting," reprinted in *Stanislavski Today*, ed. by Sonia Moore (New York: American Center for Stanislavski Theatre Art, 1973), p. 27.
43. Sonia Moore, "Vsevolod E. Meyerhold: Echoes in America," reprinted in *Stanislavski Today*, ed. by Sonia Moore (New York: American Center for Stanislavski Theatre Art, 1973), p. 106.
44. *Ibid.*, pp. 110–111.

10. The New Specialists of Movement

1. Roach, *The Player's Passion*, p. 218.
2. M. Meyers, "Moshe Feldenkrais and 'Awareness Through Movement'," *Dance Magazine* 57 (August, 1983), p. 13.
3. *Ibid.*, p. 13.
4. *Ibid.*, p. 14.
5. *Ibid.*, p. 14.
6. *Ibid.*, p. 15.
7. *Ibid.*, p. 13.
8. *Ibid.*, p. 15.
9. Sabatine, *The Actor's Image: Movement Training for Stage and Screen*, p. 26.
10. Aileen Crow, "The Alexander Technique as a Basic Approach to Theatrical

Training," reprinted in *Movement for the Actor,* ed. by Lucille S. Rubin (New York: Drama Books Specialists, 1980), p. 1.

11. *Ibid.,* p. 2.

12. *Ibid.,* pp. 2–3.

13. Sarah Barker, *The Alexander Technique: The Revolutionary Way to Use Your Body for Total Energy* (New York: Bantam Books, 1978), pp. 14–15.

14. M. Meyers, "The Alexander Technique," *Dance Magazine* 57 (August, 1983), p. 10.

15. Barker, *The Alexander Technique,* pp. 18–19.

16. Meyers, "The Alexander Technique," p. 10.

17. James H. Bierman, "The Alexander Technique Gets Directions," *Dance Scope* 12 (Spring, 1978), p. 28.

18. Barker, *The Alexander Technique,* pp. 54–55.

19. Samuel Thornton, *Laban's Theory of Movement* (Boston: Plays, Inc., 1971), p. 1.

20. Rudolf Laban, *Mastery of Movement,* ed. Lisa Ullmann (Boston: Plays, Inc., 1950), p. 1.

21. Marion North, *Personality Awareness Through Movement* (Boston: Plays, Inc., 1971), p. 4.

22. Rudolf Laban, *Choreutics* (London: MacDonald and Evans, 1966), p. viii.

23. Richard Kraus and Sarah A. Chapman, *History of the Dance in Art and Education,* 2nd ed. (Englewood Cliffs, N.J.: Prentice-Hall, 1981), p. 138.

24. Thornton, *Laban's Theory of Movement,* p. 33.

25. *Ibid.,* p. 34.

26. Laban, *The Mastery of Movement,* pp. 74–89.

27. *Ibid.,* pp. 74–75.

28. *Ibid.,* p. 104.

29. *Ibid.*

30. *Ibid.,* p. 133.

31. *Ibid.,* pp. 138–139.

32. *Ibid.,* p. 160.

33. Dr. Barbara Weber Ray, *The Reiki Factor* (Smithtown, N.Y.: Exposition Press, 1983), p. xiii.

34. *Ibid.,* p. 25.

35. Alexander Lowen, *The Way to Vibrant Health: A Manual of Bioenergetic Exercises* (New York: Harper and Row, 1977), p. 3.

36. *Ibid.*

37. *Ibid.,* p. 5.

11. The Future of Movement Training

1. Albert Mehrabian, "Communication Without Words," *Psychology Today,* September, 1968, p. 53.

2. Peter Kline and Nancy Meadows, *The Theatre Student: Physical Movement for the Theatre* (New York: Richard Rosen Press, Inc., 1971), p. 13.

3. Jerry L. Crawford, *Acting: In Person and in Style,* 3rd ed. (Dubuque, Iowa: Wm. C. Brown, 1983), p. 2.

4. Ray, *The Reiki Factor,* p. 3.

5. Crawford, *Acting,* p. 2.

6. James Turney Allen, "Greek Acting in the Fifth Century," *Classical Philology* 2, 15 (March 3, 1916), pp. 279–289.

7. *Ibid.*, pp. 286–287.

8. Walton, *The Greek Sense of Theatre*, pp. 2–3.

9. Cole and Chinoy, *Actors on Acting*, p. 19.

10. *Ibid.*, p. 20.

11. Roach, *The Player's Passion*, p. 24.

12. Cole and Chinoy, *Actors on Acting*, p. 77.

13. Diderot, *The Paradox of Acting*, p. 162.

14. *Ibid.*

15. Christine Edwards, *The Stanislavski Heritage: Its Contribution to the Russian and American Theatre* (New York: New York University Press, 1965), p. 294.

16. Sonia Moore, "The Method of Physical Actions," *Tulane Drama Review* (Summer, 1965), p. 92.

17. Hoover, *Meyerhold: The Art of Conscious Theatre*, p. 314.

18. Grotowski, *Towards a Poor Theatre*, p. 215.

19. Crawford, *Acting*, pp. 375–376.

20. Lynn Norris, "On the Training of Movement Teachers and Related Problems," *Theatre News* 11, 2 (November, 1978), p. 3.

21. *Ibid.*

22. *Ibid.*, pp. 3–4.

23. *Ibid.*, p. 4.

24. *Ibid.*

25. Jennifer Martin, "Response: UCTA Theatre Movement Supplement," *Theatre News* 11, 2 (November, 1978), p. 5.

26. *Ibid.*

27. Roger Gross, "The Promise of the New Actor Training," *Theatre News* 14, 9 (December, 1982), p. 15.

28. Jack Clay, "Self Use in Actor Training," *Tulane Drama Review* 16 (1972), p. 16.

29. *Ibid.*, p. 22.

Bibliography

Alexander, F. Matthais. *Constructive Conscious Control of the Individual,* 8th ed. London: Chaterson, 1946.
_____. *The Resurrection of the Body,* ed. Edward Marsel. New York: Dell, 1971.
Allen, James. *Greek Acting in the 5th Century.* Berkeley: University of California Press, 1916.
Aristotle. *On Man and the Universe: Poetics,* transl. Samuel Henry Butcher. Roslyn, N.Y.: Walter J. Black, 1943.
Arnold, Paul. "The Artaud Experiment." *Tulane Drama Review* (Winter, 1963).
Auslander, P. "Holy Theatre and Catharsis." *Theatre Research International* 9 (Spring, 1984), pp. 16–29.
Baker, Robyn. "An Integrated Study for the Actor's Physical Development." M.A. thesis, Baylor University, 1955.
Barker, Sarah. *The Alexander Technique.* New York: Bantam, 1978.
Barlow, Wilfred. *The Alexander Technique.* New York: Knopf, 1973.
Barnette, Dene. "The Performance Practice of Acting: The Eighteenth Century Part II: The Hands," *Theatre Research International* (1977), pp. 157–185.
_____. Part III: The Arms, *Theatre Research International* (1978), pp. 79–93.
_____. Part IV: The Eyes, the Face and the Head, *Theatre Research International* (1980), pp. 1–34.
Barrett, Marcia, et al. *Foundations for Movement.* Dubuque, Iowa: Wm. C. Brown, 1968.
Barrow, Harold M. *Man and His Movement.* Philadelphia: Lea and Febiger, 1971.
Battye, Marguerite. *Stage Movement.* Herbert Jenkins, 1954.
Benedetti, Robert. *The Actor at Work.* Englewood Cliffs, N.J.: Prentice-Hall, 1981.
Bergler, Edmund. "On Acting and Stage Fright," *Psychiatric Quarterly Supplement* 23 (1949), pp. 313–319.
Best, David, *Expression in Movement and the Arts.* Philadelphia, Pa.: Lea and Febiger, 1971.
Bieber, Margarete. *The History of the Greek and Roman Theatre.* Princeton, N.J.: Princeton University Press, 1961.
Bierman. "The Alexander Technique." *Dance Scope* 12 (Spring, 1978), pp. 24–33.
Bigsby, C.W.E. *A Critical Introduction to Twentieth Century American Drama: Beyond Broadway.* Cambridge, England: Cambridge University Press, 1985.

—————., *A Critical Introduction to Twentieth Century American Drama: 1900–1940*. Cambridge, England: Cambridge University Press, 1982.

Birdwhistle, Raymond. "Introduction to Kinesics," pamphlet. Louisville, Ky.: University of Louisville, 1957.

—————. *Kinesics and Content*. New York: Ballantine Books, 1972.

Birkhead, Mary Sue. "An Analysis of the Advanced Integration of Abilities," M.A. thesis, Baylor University, 1955.

Brecht, Bertold. "A New Technique of Acting." *Theatre Arts* 33 (January, 1949).

—————. "Notes on Stanislavsky." *Tulane Drama Review* 9 (Winter, 1964).

Brockett, Oscar G. *History of the Theatre*, 4th ed. Boston: Allyn and Bacon, 1982.

Brook, Peter. *The Empty Space*. New York: Avon Books, 1968.

Campbell, Joseph. *The Hero with a Thousand Faces*. Princeton, N.J.: Princeton University Press, 1972.

—————. *The Power of Myth*, ed. Betty Sue Flowers. New York: Doubleday, 1988.

Camryn, Walter. *An Analytical Study of Character Movement for Dancers, Actors*. New York: Dance Mart, 1959.

Carlson, Marvin. *Theories of the Theatre: A Historical and Critical Survey from the Greeks to the Present*. Ithaca, N.Y.: Cornell University Press, 1984.

Cashman, D.E. "Grotowski: Anniversary." *Theatre Journal* 31 (December, 1979), pp. 460–466.

Cassirer, Ernest. *The Philosophy of Symbolic Forms*, transl. by Ralph Manheim. New Haven: Yale University Press, 1953.

Chinoy, Helen Krich, and Cole, Toby, eds. *Actors on Acting*. New York: Crown Publishers, 1970.

Clay, Jack. "Self Use in Actor Training." *Tulane Drama Review* 16 (1972): pp. 16–22.

Cole, David. *The Theatrical Event: A Mythos, a Vocabulary, a Perspective*. Middletown, Conn.: Wesleyan University Press, 1975.

Crawford, Jerry L. *Acting: In Person and in Style*. Dubuque, Iowa: Wm. C. Brown, 1983.

Darwin, Charles. *The Expression of the Emotions in Man and Animals*. Chicago: University of Chicago Press, 1965.

Davis, Martha. *Understanding Body Movement*. New York: Arno Press, 1972.

Dell, Cecily. *A Primer for Movement Description*. New York: Dance Notation Bureau, 1970.

Delsarte, François. *Delsarte's Own Words, Being His Posthumous Writings*. New York: Werner, 1892.

—————. "Elements of the Delsarte System." Reprinted in *Actors on Acting*. New York: Crown Publishers, 1970.

Diderot, Denis. *The Paradox of Acting* [1773]. New York: Hill and Wang, 1957.

Driver, Tom F. *Romantic Quest and Modern Query*. New York: Delacorte Press, 1970.

Duerr, Edwin. *The Length and Depth of Acting*. New York: Holt, Rinehart, 1962.

Edwards, Christine. *The Stanislavski Heritage*. New York: New York University Press, 1965.

Eliade, Mircea. *Cosmos and History: The Myth of the Eternal Return*, transl. from the French by Willard R. Trask. New York: Harper Torchbooks, 1959.

Engle, Donald. "Lang's Discourse on Movement." *Educational Theatre Journal* 22, 2 (May, 1970).

Feldenkrais, Moshe. *Awareness Through Movement*. New York: Harper and Row, 1972.

_____. *Body and Mature Behavior*. New York: International University Press, 1970.

_____. *Elusive Obvious*. Meta Publishers, 1981.

_____. *The Master Move*. Meta Publishers, 1985.

_____. *The Potent Self*. New York: Harper and Row, 1985.

Fendlay, Elsa. *Rhythm and Movement, Application of Dalcroze Eurhythmics*. New York: Dance Mart, 1968.

Fenton, Jack. *Practical Movement Control*. Boston: Plays, Inc., 1969.

Findlay, R. "Grotowski's Cultural Explorations." *Theatre Journal* 32 (October, 1980), pp. 349–356.

Fishman, Morris. *The Actor in Training*. Westport, Conn.: Greenwood Press, 1961.

Forsythe, E. "Conversations with Ludwik Flazen." *Educational Theatre Journal* 30 (October, 1978), pp. 301–328.

Freund, A. "Performance from Poland." *New Republic* 155 (July 30, 1966), pp. 36–39.

Garrick, David. "An Essay on Acting." Reprinted in *Actors on Acting*. New York: Crown Publishers, 1970.

Gelb, A. "School for Stars: Actors Studio." *New York Times Magazine* (May 1, 1955), pp. 78–79.

Gherman, Y. "Meetings with Meyerhold." *Soviet Literature* 2 (1974), pp. 171–177.

Gorchahov, N.M. "Stanislavski Directs." *Saturday Review* 38 (July 9, 1955), p. 18.

Gordon, M. "Meyerhold Biomechanics." *The Drama Review* 18 (September, 1974), pp. 73–88.

Gropius, Walter. *The Theatre of the Bauhaus*. Middletown, Conn.: Weselyan University Press, 1961.

Gross, Roger. "The Promise of the New Actor Training." *Theatre News* 14, 9 (December, 1982).

Grotowski, Jerzy. *Towards a Poor Theatre*. New York: Simon and Schuster, 1968.

"Grotowski Seminar: Polish Lab Theatre." *Time Magazine* 94 (November 28, 1969), p. 71.

Gruen, J. "Towards a Poor Theatre." *Vogue* 153 (February 1, 1969), p. 132.

Hall, Edward T. *The Silent Language*. New York: Fawcett, 1966.

Hecht, Patsy Ann Clark. "Kinetic Techniques for the Actor." Ph.D. dissertation, Wayne State University, Detroit, 1971.

Hethmon, Robert, ed. *Strasberg at the Actor's Studio*. New York: Viking, 1965.

Hewes, H. "Method's Mouth: Stanislavski System." *Saturday Review* 42 (June 24, 1959), p. 25.

_____. "Wing Without Feather." *Saturday Review* 36 (July 25, 1953), pp. 26–27.

Hoffman, Theodore. "At the Grave of Stanislavski: How to Dig the Method." *Columbia University Forum* III (Winter, 1960).

Hoover, Marjorie. "Meyerhold Centennial." *The Drama Review* 18 (September, 1974), pp. 69–72.

_____. *Meyerhold: The Art of Conscious Theatre*. Amherst: University of Massachusetts Press, 1974.

Huntly, Carter. *The New Spirit in Russian Theatre*. London: Brentano's, 1929.

Ilinsky, Igor. "Biomechanics." Reprinted in *Actors on Acting*. New York: Crown Publishers, 1970.

King, Nancy. *Theatre Movement: The Actor and His Space.* New York: Drama Books Specialists, 1971.

Kitto, H.D.F. *Greek Tragedy.* New York: Harper and Row, 1976.

————. *The Greeks.* New York: Penguin, 1957.

Kline, Peter, and Meadows, Nancy. *The Theatre Student: Physical Movement for the Theatre.* New York: Richard Rosen Press, 1971.

Knott, J. "After Grotowski," transl. by Bittenek, K. *Theatre Quarterly* 10 (Summer, 1980), pp. 27–32.

Kraus, Richard, and Chapman, Sarah A. *History of the Dance in Art and Education,* 2nd ed. Englewood Cliffs, N.J.: Prentice-Hall, 1981.

Kumiega, Jennifer. *The Theatre of Grotowski.* New York: Methuen, 1985.

Laban, Rudolf. *The Language of Movement: A Guidebook to Choreutics.* Boston: Plays, Inc., 1970.

————. *The Mastery of Movement,* ed. Lisa Ullmann. Boston: Plays, Inc., 1971.

————. *Modern Educational Dance,* 2nd ed. rev. by Lisa Ullmann. New York: Frederick A. Praeger, 1968.

————. *Rudolf Laban Speaks About Movement and Dance,* ed. Lisa Ullmann. London: Laban Art of Movement Center, 1970.

Lamb, Warren. *Posture and Gesture.* London: Gerald Duckworth, 1965.

Law, A.H. "Meyerhold Speaks." *Drama Review* 18 (September 1974), pp. 108–112.

Lawler, Lilliam. *The Dance of the Ancient Greek Theatre.* University of Iowa Press, 1964.

Litvinoff, Valentina. *Use of Stanislavsky with Modern Dance.* American Dance Guild, 1972.

Lowen, Alexander. *The Way to Vibrant Health.* New York: Harper and Row, 1977.

McTeague, James H. "A New School of Dramatic Art: An Analysis of the Acting Theories and Teaching Practices of the Best Known American Acting Schools, 1875–1925." Ph.D. dissertation, State University of Iowa, 1963.

Markov, Vladimir. *Russian Futurism.* Berkeley: University of California Press, 1968.

Martin, Jennifer. "Response: UTCA Theatre Movement Supplement." *Theatre News* 11, 2 (November, 1978).

Martin, John. "How Meyerhold Trains His Actors." *Theatre Guild Magazine* 7 (November, 1930).

Mehrabian, Albert. "Communication Without Words." *Psychology Today* (September, 1968).

Metheny, Eleanor, *Movement and Meaning.* New York: McGraw, 1968.

Meyerhold, Vsevolod. *Body Dynamics.* New York: McGraw, 1952.

————. *Meyerhold on Theatre,* ed. and trans. by Edward Braun. New York: Hill and Wang, 1969.

————. "On the Theatre." *Tulane Drama Review* 7 (May, 1960).

Moody, C. "Meyerhold and the Commedia dell'Arte." *Modern Language Review* 73 (October, 1978), pp. 859–869.

Moore, Sonia. "The Method of Physical Actions." *Tulane Drama Review* (Summer, 1965), pp. 91–94.

————. *Stanislavski Today.* New York: New York Center for Stanislavski Theatre Art, 1973.

————. *Training An Actor,* rev. ed. New York: Penguin Books, 1979.

Morowitz, C. "Meyerhold Alone." *Contemporary Review* 240 (April, 1982), pp. 208–212.

Myers, M. "Alexander Technique." *Dance Magazine* 57 (August, 1983), pp. BT 9–11.

_____. "Body Therapy." *Dance Magazine* 54 (April, 1980), pp. 90–92.

_____. "Moshe Feldenkrais." *Dance Magazine* 57 (August, 1983), pp. BT 13–15.

Nicholls, Bronwen. *Move!*. Boston: Plays, Inc., 1972.

Norris, Lynn. "On the Training of Movement Teachers and Related Problems." *Theatre News* 11, 2 (November, 1978).

North, Marion. *Personality Assessment Through Movement*. Boston: Plays, Inc., 1975.

Olf, J.M. "Acting and Being." *Theatre Journal* 33 (March, 1981), pp. 34–45.

Oxenford, Lyn. *Playing Period Plays*. London: Coach House Press, 1959.

Peck, S. "Temple of the Method." *New York Times Magazine* (May 6, 1956), pp. 26–27.

Penrod, Joseph. *Movement for the Performing Artist*. Palo Alto, Calif.: Mayfield Publ. Co., 1974.

Pisk, Liz. *The Actor and His Body*. New York: Theatre Arts Books, 1975.

Poggi, Jack. "Second Thoughts on the Theory of Action." Printed in *Actor Training*, ed. by Richard Brown. New York: Drama Books, 1976.

Randall, M. *Basic Movement*. London: G. Bell, 1961.

Ray, Barbara Weber. *The Reiki Factor*. Smithtown, N.Y.: Exposition Press, 1983.

Reich, Wilhelm. *Character Analysis*. London: Vision Press, 1971.

Richards, Kenneth, and Thomason, Peter, ed. *The Eighteenth Century English Stage*. New York: Harper and Row, 1972.

Richardson, Tony. "An Account of the Actors Studio." *Sight and Sound* 26 (Winter, 1956–57).

Roach, Joseph. *The Player's Passion: Studies in the Science of Acting*. Newark: University of Delaware Press, 1985.

Rolph, Ida P. *Structural Integration*. San Francisco: San Francisco Guild for Structural Study, 1980.

Rubin, Lucille S., ed. *Movement for the Actor*. New York: Drama Books Specialists, 1980.

Russell, Douglas A. *Period Style for the Theatre*, 2nd ed. Boston: Allyn and Bacon, 1987.

Sabatine, Jean. *The Actor's Image: Movement Training for Stage and Screen*. Collaborator, David Hodges. Englewood Cliffs, N.J.: Prentice-Hall, 1983.

Sayler, Oliver. *Inside the Moscow Art Theatre*. New York: Brentano's, 1925.

Schechner, Richard. "An Interview with Grotowski." *Tulane Drama Review* 13 (Fall, 1968), p. 32.

Schmidt, P. "Director Works with Playwright." *Educational Theatre Journal* 29 (May, 1977), pp. 214–220.

Schmidt, Paul, ed. *Meyerhold at Work*. Austin: University of Texas Press, 1979.

Schoop, Trudy. *Won't You Join the Dance?* Palo Alto, Calif.: National Press Books, 1974.

Seidelman, A. "Movement and the Actor." *After Dark* 13, 8 (December, 1970), pp. 40–41.

Shawn, Ted. *Every Little Movement*. New York: Dance Horizons, 1968.

Shayon, R.L. "Method or Madness?" *Saturday Review* 39 (February 18, 1956), p. 26.

Smart, Alista. "Dramatic Gesture and Expression in the Age of Hogarth." *Apollo* 82 (1965), pp. 90–97.

Smith, Hope M. *Introduction to Human Movement*. Addison-Wesley, 1968.

Sorell, Walter. "We Work Towards Freedom." *Dance Magazine* 38 (January, 1964).

Stanislavski, Constantin. *Building a Character*, transl. by Elizabeth Reynolds Hapgood. New York: Theatre Arts Books, 1949.

_____. *Creating a Role*, transl. by Elizabeth Reynolds Hapgood. New York: Theatre Arts Books, 1949.

_____. "Leaves from Stanislavski: Notebook Excerpts from Konstantin Stanislavski." *Unesco Courier* 16 (November, 1963), pp. 20–22.

_____. *My Life in Art*, transl. by J.J.Robbins. New York: Theatre Arts Books, 1948.

_____. "Stanislavski and the Teaching of Dramatic Art." *World Theatre* 7, 1 (1959).

Strasberg, Lee. "The Magic of Meyerhold." *New Theatre* 1 (September, 1934).

Styan, J.L. *Drama, Stage and Audience*. New York: Cambridge University Press, 1975.

Symons, James. *Meyerhold's Theatre of the Grotesque*. Coral Gables, Fla.: University of Miami Press, 1971.

Thornton, Samuel. *Laban's Theory of Movement*. Boston: Plays, Inc., 1971.

Todd, Mabel. *The Thinking Body*. New York: Dance Horizons, 1937.

Ullmann, Lisa, ed. *Laban Speaks Out About Movement and Dance*. London: Laban Art Movement Center, 1970.

Valency, Maurice. *The End of the World: An Introduction to Contemporary Drama*. New York: Oxford University Press, 1980.

von Kleist, Heinrich. "On the Marionette Theatre." *Tulane Drama Review* 16 (T-55, 1972), pp. 22–26.

Walton, Michael. *The Greek Sense of Tragedy*. New York: Methuen, 1984.

Wasserman, Earl. "The Sympathetic Imagination of 18th Century Theories of Acting." *Journal of English and German Philology* 47 (1947), pp. 264–272.

Westfeldt, Leslie. *F. Matthais Alexander: The Man and His Work*. New York: Assoc. Bookseller, 1964.

Wildeblood, Joan. *The Polite World*. London: Davis-Poynter, 1973.

Wiles, Timothy J. *The Theatre Event: Modern Theories of Performance*. Chicago: University of Chicago Press, 1980.

Williams, C. "Giants—Meyerhold." *Drama* 134 (Autumn, 1979), pp. 46–52.

Willis, Ronald. "The American Lab Theatre." *Tulane Drama Review* (Fall, 1964), pp. 112–116.

Wolff, Charlotte. *A Psychology of Gesture*. New York: Arno Press, 1972.

Woodbury, Lael. "The Externalization of Emotion." *Educational Theatre Journal* (October, 1969), pp. 177–183.

Worthen, William B. *The Idea of the Actor*. Princeton, N.J.: Princeton University Press, 1984.

Index

Abstraction 75, 113, 132
Absurdist drama 127
Absurdist movement 67–68
Active culture vs. passive culture
    69, 78
Actor's Studio 130
Adler, Stella 48
Aeschylus 98
Aesop 18
Alexander, F.M. 49, 88, 94–99, 103,
    107, 118–120, 122–123, 128, 132;
    "Body Awareness," 97–98; Tech-
    nique xii, 3, 88–89, 94–99, 111,
    125–126, 129, 131
Andronicus, Livius 18
Apollo 19
Appia 54, 73
Aristophanes 9
Aristotle 45, 78, 114; *Poetics* 9–11,
    14, 18
Artaud 31, 44, 49, 65, 73, 118
Artaudian theatre 71
Artistic kleptomania 65
Athenian theatre 14
Autoperformance 70
Avant-Garde 61, 63, 82, 127
"Awareness Through Movement"
    92–93

Ballet 3, 52
Barrault, Jean-Louis 71

"Basic Movement" 98
Bekhterev, Vladimir 59
Biblical drama 24
Bioenergetics 88, 105–106, 111, 119,
    131
Biomechanics 53, 56–57, 61–63,
    79–81, 84–85, 118–119
Blok, Alexander 56
"Body Integration" 95
"Body Work" 86
Boleslavsky, Richard 48
Bread and Puppet Theatre 104
Brecht, Bertold 34, 119
Brook, Peter 68, 75

Cabotin 53
Catharsis 72, 75–76
Cathartic release 12
Chaikin, Joseph 82, 119, 131
Chekhov, Anton 52
Choreutics 100
Christianity 23
Cicero 20
Clurman, Harold 48
Combat skills 120
Commedia dell'Arte 57, 114
Communist Party 54
Constructivism 56, 60–61
Copeau 75

Craig, Gordon 56, 71, 72
Cubism 56

Dadism 56
Dalcroze 61, 74
Dark Ages 21
Darwin 38, 45
Darwinism 30, 43
Decorum 26–27, 114
Delsarte, François xiii, 35, 38–41, 63,
  74, 116–117, 119, 128; Delsarte's
  System, 39–40; Delsarte's three
  zones, 39
Diderot, Denis 27, 31–34, 44–45, 61,
  87, 92, 94, 114–116, 119
Diderot's legacy 34
Dionysus 9
Divine neutral 107
Dramatic ritual 10
Duke of Saxe-Meiningen 34
Duncan, Isadora 51

Effort/Shape 3, 100
Efforts 101, 103
Elizabethan actor 24–25, 114
Elizabethan period 21, 114–115
Emmeleia 12
Emotion memory 46
The Empty Space 75
English Renaissance 21
Enlightenment 37
Etude 57
Eurhythmics 61
Euripides 9

Fabula ricinata 19
Fabula saltica 20
Facial mask 74
Feldenkrais, Moshe 49, 88–95, 99,
  107, 111, 118–119, 122–123,
  125–126, 128, 131–132 "Body
  Awareness" xiii, 88, 92; Body
  Integration 88; Feldenkrais's
  method 90–93

Fencing 3, 25, 61, 104
Festival of Dionysus 9
Flazen, Ludwik 67
Fonteyn, Dame Margot xii
Freud 43, 45
Futurism 56
Futurists 34, 76

Garrick, David 27, 29–31, 116–117
Gastev, A.K. 59
Gesture 11, 25, 37, 39, 120, 123
Given circumstances 34
Graham, Martha 113
Greek actor 12–13, 112
Greek theatre 12, 112, 127
Gropius, Walter 51
Grotesque absurdism 68
Grotowski, Jerzy xiii, 14, 31, 35, 44,
  65–80, 82–87, 118–119, 130–132;
  style of "poor theatre," 69, 104,
  119; trance theory 76

Happenings 73, 104
Hauptmann 41
Hawkins, Erick 88
Holm, Hanya 88
Holy actor 75–76, 79
Holy Theatre 76
Horace 18

Ibsen, Henrik 41
Ideograms 75
Illud tempus 75
Impressionist 53
Impressionist Theatre 53
Improvisation 17, 47, 69, 73, 104
Industrial Revolution 43
Industrialism 37
Institute of the Actor 69
Ionesco 66

James, William 59
Jazz dance 3

Karate 3
Kinesthetic memory 48

Laban, Rudolf von 49, 88, 99–104, 107, 111, 119–120, 128; effort/shape theory xiii, 88–89, 100, 126, 130, 132
Labonotation 100
Lascaux, France xi, 8
Lenin 58
Lessac 125
Linklater 125
Living Theatre 104
Louis, Murray 131
Louis XIV 29
Lowen, Alexander 49, 106, 120, 128–129
Lucian 19, 113

Machine for acting 56
MacKaye, James Steele 39
Maeterlinck 54–56
Marceau, Marcel 67
Marionette 60, 71
Marlowe, Christopher 68
Martin, John 62–63
Mask 12–13, 41, 78
Matrix 47
Mehrabian, Dr. Albert 109
Method actor 48, 104
Method of physical actions 46–47, 49, 79–80, 84–85, 117
Meyerhold, Vsevolod xiii, 34–35, 44, 49, 51, 62, 66, 71, 73, 79–82 84, 87, 110–111, 118–119; Constructivism 56, 66; method of acting training 63; Theory of Biomechanics 55, 58, 60, 80–81, 110–111, 131
Middle Ages 23
Mime 3, 17, 19
Mimesis 10–11, 32
Mimetic dance 11
Modern ballet 14
Modern dance 3, 61, 88

Moore, Sonia 48
Moscow Art Theatre 34, 46, 52–53
Movement for actors 120, 131
Movement patterns 6
Movement specialists 2, 119–122
Movement training 3, 119
Multiple consciousness 47
Muscle memory 34
Mystery and morality plays 24
Myth 7

Naturalism 30, 48, 55
Naturalistic theatre 56
Negative exercises 73
Nemirovich-Danchenko, Vladimir 46, 52, 54
Neoclassicism 115
Neuro-linguistic 88, 131
Neurophysiology 90
Nikolais, Alwin 131

Open Theatre 104
Opera 52
Oriental theatre 44, 60, 77
Oriental training 119, 131

Pantomime 19, 62
Paradox of Acting 31, 34, 115
Paratheatrical work 77
Pathos 18
Pavlov 45, 59
Physical actions 48
Physical rhythm 45
Physicalization 88
Pisk, Liz 120, 128
Plastic arts 31
Plautus 24
Polish Laboratory Theatre 14, 65, 67–70, 73
Poor Theatre 68, 71, 75–76, 80, 82, 118
Positivism 116
Posturing 30

Primitive ritual 5
Psychic impulses 46
Psycho-drama 77
Psychological gesture 34
Public Solitude 46

Quintillian xiii, 18, 20, 25, 29,
    113–114

Rationalism 37
Realistic acting 29
Reflection 33
Reflexology 59
Reiki 88, 105, 111, 131
Rey, Barbara Weber 105
Rhetorical acting 29–31
Rhythm 69
Rhythm-tempo 45–46
Rich theatre 75
Rise of women's movement 43
Rite 6
Rites of Passage 6
Ritual 5–6, 8
Ritualistic actions 7
Ritualistic dance 5
Rolf, Ida 49
Rolfing 3
Roman actor 17, 113
Roman comedy 114
Roman orchestra 20
Romanticism 30
Russian Realism 55
Russian Revolution 53–54

Schemata 12
Secular Holiness 75
Self-actualization 79
Seneca 24
Shakespeare 24, 115, 126; Hamlet, 25
Sixteen Etudes 57
Socialist Realism 55, 67
Solidarity 69
Soloviev, Vladimir N. 57

Sophocles 9
Soviet Taylorist 58
Stage combat 3
Stage movement 124
Stalin 54
Stanislavski, Constantin xiii, 31, 33,
    35, 44–49, 51–55, 63, 66, 70,
    73–74, 78–80, 82, 84, 87, 94,
    110–111, 116–117, 127, 132; method
    45, 48, 77, 117, 119, 130–131;
    system 44–46, 48–49, 68, 71, 79,
    84–85
Stock acting 20
Strasberg, Lee 48, 83, 130
Stravinsky, Igor 51
Strindberg 41
Sublime 37
Surrealism 56
Symbolism 53, 56
Symbolist 52
Symbolist Movement 52
Symbolist Theatre 53

Taboo 6
t'ai chi 3, 104, 111, 129, 131
t'ai kuan do 111
Taylor, Frederick W. 58
Taylorism 58, 60
Teliakovsky, V.A. 53
Terence 24
Theatre movement 120, 128
Theatre of the Absurd 61, 73
Theatre of the Thirteen Rows 67, 69
Theatricalization of movement 15
Theatron 13
Todd's Body Mechanics 899
Tomaschevski mime 89
Towards a Poor Theatre 71, 82
Trance acting 111
Translumination 72

Uber-marionettes 71
Units and Objectives 46
University departments 123

Vakhtangov 66
Verhaeren, Emile 56
Verisimilitude 19, 41

Wagner 54
Western Absurdism 68
Wilkiewicz, Stanislav 68
Willing suspension of disbelief 53
Women's Movement 43

"Work actions" 102
Work in progress 82

Yoga 89–90, 94, 104, 111, 122, 131

Zen 65
Zero position 94